THIS IS BRANDING

*THE SHORTCUT TO BUILDING A BRAND
PEOPLE LOVE AND GROWING YOUR BUSINESS*

KAREE LAING

Published by Staten House (statenhouse.com)
7887 San Felipe Dr. Suite 122
Houston TX 77063

Editing by Alicia Williams
Book cover by Elizabeth Tenorio

First Edition 2024

Hardcover ISBN: **979-8-89587-337-3**
Softcover ISBN: **979-8-89587-335-9**
Audiobook ISBN: **979-8-89587-331-1**

ThisIsBrandingBook.com
Printed in United States

(S)

Staten House

Download the Audiobook for FREE!

Thank you for purchasing *This is Branding*! As a special bonus, I'm excited to offer you the **audiobook version** of the book **completely free**. Whether you're on the go, at the gym, or commuting, you can now take these powerful branding insights with you, wherever you are!

Here's How to Download Your Free Audiobook:
1. **Visit:** ThisIsBrandingBook.com/audio
2. **Enter Your Purchase Info:** Fill in your order details from the book purchase to unlock your free download.
3. **Download the Audiobook:** Choose your preferred audio format, download, and enjoy!
4. **Start Listening:** Play it on your favorite device anytime, anywhere.

Why Download the Audiobook?
- **Convenience:** Get the same actionable strategies and inspiration while multitasking—whether you're driving, exercising, or relaxing at home.
- **Immersive Learning:** Listening brings a different, more personal dynamic to the material. Hearing the tone and emphasis can help key concepts stick even better.
- **Boost Your Branding Knowledge:** The audio format allows you to easily revisit chapters, catch new insights, and deepen your understanding at your own pace.

Take advantage of this **exclusive free offer**—unlock the audiobook now and get ready to take your brand-building journey to the next level!

ThisIsBrandingBook.com/audio

DEDICATION

To the dreamers, creators, and entrepreneurs who dare to build something meaningful, this book is for you—may it inspire you to turn your vision into a brand that leaves a lasting impact. This book is dedicated to those who believe in the power of their vision, who embrace the challenges and celebrate the victories along the way. May your journey be filled with growth, resilience, and the courage to create a brand that reflects your passion and purpose.

And to my family and friends—your unwavering support and belief in me has been my greatest inspiration. Thank you for always pushing me to dream bigger.

TABLE OF CONTENTS

Entrepreneurs, this is your call to build a brand that doesn't just sell—but inspires, leads, and transforms; the world is waiting for your story, so make it unforgettable.

ACKNOWLEDGMENTS

Writing this book has been a journey of discovery, reflection, and focus—one that I could not have completed without the support and encouragement of many incredible people.

First and foremost, I want to thank my family. Your belief in me, even when the path seemed uncertain, has been my greatest source of strength. To my closest friends, your encouragement and feedback kept me grounded and motivated throughout this process.

I'd also like to thank my clients, past and present, for trusting me with your brands and allowing me to be part of your growth stories. Each of you has shaped my understanding of what it means to build a brand that matters, a brand with heart and soul.

To the mentors and colleagues who have guided me along the way—your wisdom and advice have been invaluable. I am deeply grateful for your insights and the inspiration you've provided throughout my career. To my team, without you nothing would be possible. You guys ROCK!

Finally, to the readers of this book—thank you for joining me on this journey. I hope the lessons and strategies within these pages help you create a brand that inspires, connects, and leaves a lasting impact. But most importantly, one that brings you great success and money too ☺ . Here's to you!

INTRODUCTION

In a crowded garage in California, a young man sits hunched over a makeshift workbench, tinkering with wires and circuit boards. It's 1976, and Steve Jobs, along with his friend Steve Wozniak, is on the verge of creating something that would revolutionize the way people interact with technology. What they didn't know at the time was that this humble garage would soon become legendary. It wasn't just the birth of a computer; it was the birth of a brand that would change the world.

The early Apple computers weren't just pieces of hardware; they represented a new way of thinking—about technology, design, and the future. People didn't just buy Apple products; they became part of a movement, a way of thinking. Over time, Apple wasn't just selling computers, phones, or music players. It was selling an idea: that technology could be beautiful, simple, and personal. Apple became a symbol of innovation, creativity, and individuality. And just like that garage, the brand itself became legendary.

But why Apple? There were countless tech companies in the 1970s and 1980s, all creating innovative products.

What made Apple different? Why did it stand out, while other companies with equally impressive technology faded into the background?

The answer lies not in the product itself, but in the story Apple told, the meaning behind the brand. Apple wasn't just a company—it was a vision, a belief system that people wanted to be a part of. When you bought an Apple product, you weren't just buying a computer or a phone. You were buying into the idea that technology could empower creativity, that it could be simple yet groundbreaking. And most importantly, you were buying into a sense of identity—Apple wasn't for everyone, it was for those who dared to think different.

This is the essence of powerful branding. It's not about having the best product on the shelf or the sleekest design—it's about the story you tell and the connection you create with your audience. Brands that people love are the ones that make their customers feel something. Apple made people feel like they were part of a revolution, part of something that was changing the world.

So how does a brand like Apple inspire this kind of loyalty, while others with great products fail to connect on that same level? It comes down to something deeper than marketing or advertising. It's about creating a brand that people believe in.

In this book, I'll guide you through the process of building a brand that people don't just purchase from—they believe in. A brand that resonates with them on a personal level. By building a brand based on beliefs, rather than just the benefits or features it offers, you allow your customers to invest in an aspirational future—one that includes you. We'll explore the key elements of what I call the "**Brand Belief System,"** which consists of seven essential components:

- √ **The Origin Story** – Every great brand has a story about where it came from. For Apple, it was the garage. For your brand, it might be something different, but the key is making it meaningful.
- √ **The Purpose** – What does your brand stand for? Apple stands for creativity, innovation, and simplicity.
- √ **The Symbols** – Apple's iconic logo, the sleek design of their products—these symbols are instantly recognizable and evoke the brand's identity.
- √ **The Routines** – How do people interact with your brand in their daily lives? Whether it's using an iPhone or a MacBook, Apple products became part of their users' routines.
- √ **The Opponents** – What does your brand stand against? Apple positioned itself as the brand for the rebels, the thinkers, and the creators—against the mainstream.
- √ **The Language** – Apple's marketing campaigns have always been simple yet profound, from "Think Different" to the minimalist product names.
- √ **The Visionary** – Steve Jobs wasn't just the CEO of Apple; he was the face and spirit of the brand. He embodied everything Apple stood for.

These seven elements form the foundation of a brand that goes beyond a product—it creates a belief system. And when people believe in a brand, they stay loyal to it. They become part of a community, part of something bigger than just a transaction.

Throughout this book, I'll show you how to build these elements into your brand. We'll explore **"This is Branding Examples"** that show how brands have mastered this art of building a connection and driving business growth, and how you can apply the same principles to create a brand that not only stands out but becomes a meaningful part of people's lives.

But before we go any further, let's define a few key branding theories that are core elements to your overall understanding.

Branding is one of the most critical aspects of building a successful business, yet it's often misunderstood or oversimplified. Many people think of branding as just a logo or a catchy slogan, but in reality, it's much deeper and more strategic. Branding is the process of creating a unique identity for a business in the minds of consumers. It's about telling a story, evoking emotions, and ultimately building trust and loyalty with your audience. So, it's important that before we discuss the key branding belief structure, we explore the foundational concepts of branding, discuss key theories, and look at how brands apply these ideas in practice.

WHAT IS BRANDING?

At its core, branding is the deliberate effort to create a **perception** of your business in the minds of your audience. It's how customers recognize, experience, and feel about your products or services. Branding goes beyond logos and taglines; it includes everything from your company's mission and values to customer experience, visual identity, and messaging.

Brand: A brand is the **identity** of a business, product, or individual, including the emotional and psychological relationship between the business and its customers. It's what people think of when they hear your name, see your logo, or use your product.

Branding: The **process** of shaping that identity in the minds of your customers. It includes defining what makes your business unique, how you deliver value, and how you communicate to your audience.

WHY BRANDING MATTERS

Branding is a crucial process for both new and established businesses because it creates a sense of identity and differentiation for your products or services. In a crowded marketplace, strong branding helps you stand out, develop customer loyalty, and drive business growth. Customers don't just buy products—they buy the **emotions** and **experiences** attached to them.

- √ **Recognition and Awareness**: A strong brand makes your business instantly recognizable and memorable. This can be achieved through consistent use of visual elements, messaging, and tone.
- √ **Trust and Credibility**: A well-crafted brand builds trust. Customers are more likely to engage with a business that appears professional, consistent, and aligned with their values.
- √ **Emotional Connection**: A brand that resonates emotionally can turn one-time customers into

lifelong brand advocates. This emotional connection is built through storytelling, values, and a strong brand purpose.

KEY BRANDING CONCEPTS AND THEORIES

1) Brand Identity

This is how **you** want your brand to be perceived. It's the collection of all the visual and verbal elements (logo, color scheme, messaging, etc.) that represents your business.
Example: **Coca-Cola**'s identity is built on happiness, refreshment, and sharing joyful moments. This is conveyed consistently through their red color, dynamic logo, and positive messaging.

2) Brand Image

This is how **customers** perceive your brand. While you can control your brand identity, brand image is shaped by your customers' experiences and perceptions. Ensuring that your brand identity aligns with your customers' image of you and/or your business is key to building a strong brand.
Example: **Uber**'s brand identity emphasizes convenience and innovation, but its brand image has occasionally fluctuated due to customer service concerns or regulatory issues. Ensuring that identity and image align is crucial for Uber to maintain trust.

3) Brand Equity

Brand equity refers to the **value** your brand adds to your business beyond physical assets or products. Strong brand equity means your customers are willing to pay more, remain loyal, and recommend your brand to others.

Positive Brand Equity: This is built when customers have positive experiences with your brand, associate it with quality, and trust it.

Example: **Apple** has significant brand equity. People are willing to pay a premium for Apple products because of the association with innovation, design, and user experience.

Negative Brand Equity: If your brand has a history of poor customer service or product failures, you could develop negative brand equity, which harms your reputation and sales.

4) The Brand Archetype Theory

Brand archetypes, based on Carl Jung's theory of universal archetypes, suggest that brands can take on distinct personalities that tap into fundamental human motivations and emotions. These archetypes are rooted in the collective unconscious—shared human experiences that transcend culture and time. By aligning a brand with a specific archetype, businesses can create emotionally resonant connections with their audience, making their message feel familiar and personally relevant.

While not always the first tool marketers turn to, brand archetypes are powerful for companies that want to create strong, emotionally connected branding. These archetypes give brands a deeper personality, helping them speak to universal desires like freedom, security, adventure, and belonging. By leveraging these symbolic characters, brands can shape how people perceive them on a subconscious level, building trust and loyalty more effectively.

The 12 Common Brand Archetypes

Here's an overview of the three most widely recognized brand archetypes and how they are used in branding:

√ **The Hero**: Brands that inspire customers to strive for personal greatness by overcoming challenges. These brands often emphasize empowerment, achievement, strength, and resilience.
Example: Nike – The "Just Do It" slogan encourage s people to push beyond their limits and embrace their inner strength.

√ **The Innocent**: Brands that focus on simplicity, purity, and optimism. They often represent values like honesty, safety, and wholesomeness, which appeals to customers who value natural beauty or straight-forwardness.
Example: Dove – With its focus on natural beauty and body positivity, Dove promotes the message of self-love and purity.

√ **The Explorer**: Brands that promote freedom, adventure, and discovery. These brands speak to the desire to explore the unknown and break away from routine, encouraging independence and self-discovery.
Example: Jeep – With its rugged, adventurous image, Jeep embodies the spirit of the outdoors and the thrill of discovery, appealing to those who seek to venture off the beaten path.

Each archetype provides a **framework** for shaping a brand's identity, messaging, and customer experience. By aligning with a specific archetype, brands can consistently deliver experiences that resonate emotionally and stand the test of time.

PRACTICAL APPLICATIONS OF BRANDING IN BUSINESS

Branding isn't just theoretical—it's deeply practical. Let's look at how brands have applied these concepts to create a real-world impact.

Creating a Brand Strategy

Your brand strategy defines how, what, where, when, and to whom you communicate your brand's message. It's your **roadmap** for building a brand that not only stands out but resonates with your target audience. A solid brand strategy includes:

- √ **Target Audience**: Understand who your customers are, what they care about, and how your brand can meet their needs.
- √ **Brand Positioning**: This is how you differentiate yourself from the competition. It's about finding the sweet spot where your brand stands out. **Example: Tesla** is positioned as the leader in electric vehicles, blending innovation with sustainability.
- √ **Brand Messaging**: Clearly articulate your brand's voice, tone, and key messages. What do you want customers to know about your brand? How should they feel when they interact with you? **Example: Patagonia's** messaging revolves around environmental activism and ethical consumerism, aligning its products with its mission to protect the planet.

The Importance of Consistency

Consistency is key to branding success. Your brand must be consistent in visual identity, tone, messaging, and customer experience across all touchpoints, including your website, social media, advertising, and in-store experiences. A consistent brand builds trust, authority, and recognition.

Example: McDonald's uses consistent visual elements like the golden arches and the same color palette across the globe. Whether in New York or Tokyo, customers recognize the brand instantly.

Building a Brand Community

Modern branding extends beyond customer loyalty—it's about creating a **community**. It's no surprise that brands that foster community around shared values or interests see higher engagement and stronger emotional bonds with their customers.

Example: LEGO created a thriving community of fans through their interactive platforms, social media, and user-generated content, allowing customers to feel like part of a creative family.

Branding is more than aesthetics though—it's about shaping the relationship between your business and your customers. By focusing on creating a strong brand identity, aligning it with your customers' perceptions, and consistently delivering on your brand promise, you can build a brand that stands the test of time.

In this book, we'll go deeper into how to craft and execute a powerful branding strategy. You'll learn how to define your brand's beliefs, connect emotionally with your audience, and measure your brand's success to ensure you're building long-term equity in the marketplace. Branding is not just what you sell, it's who you are and what you stand for.

SO, WHAT WILL YOU GET FROM THIS BOOK?

~~This book will teach you to be great!~~ No, it will not. The truth is that you either **already have greatness within you, or you don't.** What this book *will* do is help you unlock that greatness by showing you how to harness the power of branding to express it, whether for yourself or for your business. It will guide you through building a brand that reflects your authentic self, connects deeply with your audience, and stands out in a world full of noise. You'll learn the tools, strategies, and mindset needed to take what's already inside you—and amplify it through bold, impactful branding.

This isn't about formulas or quick fixes. It's about discovering your unique voice, crafting a story that resonates, and creating a brand that feels both meaningful and memorable. You won't just build a business or a product—you'll build something that people believe in. And that's where the real magic happens.

Because after all, branding isn't just about logos, color palettes, or catchy slogans—it's the very essence of what makes a business stand out, resonate with its audience, and drive long-term success. For entrepreneurs and small business owners, building a strong brand is crucial to breaking through the noise of today's crowded market. But branding can also feel overwhelming if you're unsure of where to begin. That's why this book is designed to simplify the process and help you think like a branding expert, no matter where you are in your entrepreneurial journey.

This book is your roadmap to creating a standout brand that not only captures attention but also fosters loyalty and drives growth. Whether you're an entrepreneur just starting out or a small business owner looking to refine your brand's presence, you'll find actionable strategies to help you define your brand identity, build consistency, and leverage powerful branding techniques that lead to real results. **You'll learn how to:**

√ Develop a clear brand identity that differentiates you from your competitors.

√ Craft a personal brand that resonates with your audience and builds trust.

√ Ensure consistency across all your branding efforts, both online and offline.

√ Use brand psychology to tap into emotions and create meaningful connections.

√ Tell your brand's story in a way that engages and captivates your audience.

√ Harness the power of AI to enhance your branding and improve customer experiences.

By the end of this book, you'll have the tools and confidence to think like a branding expert and create a business that not only stands out but also thrives.

Branding is often misunderstood as something that only large corporations need to worry about. However, for small businesses and entrepreneurs, branding is just as, if not more, important. Your brand is your business' identity—

it's what people think of when they hear your name, see your logo, or interact with your products or services.

Here's why branding matters for your business:
- √ **First Impressions Count:** In a world where customers have endless options, a strong brand helps you make an unforgettable first impression. It's your chance to visually and emotionally connect with your audience before they've even interacted with your product or service.
- √ **Differentiation in a Crowded Market:** No matter what industry you're in, competition is fierce. A strong brand sets you apart by clearly communicating what makes your business unique.
- √ **Building Trust and Loyalty:** Consistent branding fosters trust, and trust is the foundation of customer loyalty. When your customers trust your brand, they are more likely to become repeat buyers and advocates for your business.
- √ **Emotional Connection:** People don't just buy products; they buy emotions, experiences, and stories. A well-crafted brand taps into your audience's emotions, creating a connection that goes beyond the transactional.

For entrepreneurs and small business owners, branding is the key to standing out, gaining loyal customers, and creating a business that thrives long-term.

My Journey from Branding Beginner to Expert
My name is Karee Laing, and I'm an accidental entrepreneur. After graduating from law school, I took an unconventional path and decided to move to Houston, Texas, to pursue a career that blended creativity with the

analytical. That journey led me to the design/build industry, where I first discovered the power of branding. I witnessed how effective branding—through visuals, storytelling, and emotion—could set companies apart in even the most competitive and oversaturated markets.

It wasn't long before I started my first business, and it was branding that made me stand out. The visual curiosity I developed in the design/build industry easily transferred into visual storytelling, and that's when my career in branding truly began. I started a marketing agency, and our first big break came with a large branding project for an oil and gas company. From that point forward, branding became second nature to me. Since then, I have spoken on branding, hosted workshops, led a team to wining over 100 industry awards, and led branding projects for small start-ups to some of the largest institutions in the country.

Our award-wining agency has crafted brands for businesses across multiple industries. We've be recognized many times for our work, but the real reward is knowing how many businesses we've helped grow and thrive through effective branding. Whether it's telling a story, tapping into emotions, crafting the customer's journey visually, or being authentically you—these are the elements that make branding so powerful.

Now, it's important to remember that branding is woven into everything we do. We figured out how to sell with visuals, connect with customers through storytelling, and create authentic brands that resonate. In this book, I'm excited to share everything I've learned so that you, too, can build a brand that stands out, connects with your audience, and drives long-term success.

My Personal Philosophy: Branding is Life
I believe branding is more than just a business tool—it's a reflection of life itself. Just like in life, your brand evolves as you grow. Think of branding as a journey of self-discovery for your business, where every experience, challenge, and success shapes your identity. Much like the personal values we hold dear in our lives, your brand's values should be at the core of everything you do. Your brand, like your character, should be authentic, consistent, and rooted in what you stand for.

Life is about the connections we make, the stories we share, and the impact we leave behind. Branding is no different. A strong brand connects with people on an emotional level, tells a compelling story, and creates a lasting impression that resonates far beyond a product or service. Just as we navigate life with intention, every decision you make in your branding journey should be purposeful and aligned with your ultimate vision.

Whether you're building a brand or crafting your life's journey, the same principles apply-be authentic, be consistent, and always aim to leave a lasting, positive impact.

Need Help with Branding? Let's Talk
As you move through this book, you'll find plenty of actionable advice and strategies to help you create a standout brand on your own. But if you ever feel stuck, or if you're ready to take your branding to the next level, I'm here to help.

My team and I have helped hundreds of businesses transform their brands into powerful assets that drive growth and build loyalty. If you're looking for personalized guidance or need expert help to implement the strategies you're learning in this book, don't hesitate to reach out.

You can connect with me directly at karee@kareelaing.com or through my personal calendar here: *kareelaing.com/calendar*. Whether you need a consultation, a full rebrand, or ongoing branding support, we'll work with you to create something that not only stands out but also drives real results.

HOW TO USE THIS BOOK

This book is designed to be your guide on the journey to building a powerful, standout brand. Whether you're an entrepreneur, small business owner, or creative professional, the following chapters are filled with strategies, insights, and exercises that will equip you to think like a branding expert. But to truly transform your business, you'll need more than just knowledge—you'll need to take action. That's why this book is structured to help you apply what you learn in real-time.

Let's look at how you can get the most value from this book and ensure that you're implementing the strategies effectively.

How to Get the Most Out of This Book

This book is meant to be interactive, engaging, and above all, practical. It's not just about reading and absorbing information; it's about applying these lessons to your business and seeing real results. Here's how to make sure you're getting the most out of each chapter:

- √ **Don't Rush Through**: Take your time with each chapter. Branding is a journey, not a quick fix. While it's tempting to skim through the content, try to fully engage with each concept. Pause after each section, reflect on how it applies to your business, and act on what you've learned.

- √ **Take Notes**: As you go through each chapter, jot down key takeaways and insights that resonate with you. This will help you internalize the information and give you a personalized reference guide to revisit when you need it.

- √ **Apply Each Concept in Real-Time**: The exercises and prompts provided are designed to help you take immediate action. Don't wait until you've finished the entire book—start implementing the strategies right away. You'll see greater progress when you apply the concepts while they're fresh in your mind.

- √ **Return to the Book as Needed**: Building a brand isn't a one-and-done process. As your business grows and evolves, you may want to revisit certain chapters or exercises. This book is a resource you can return to whenever you need guidance or inspiration on your branding journey.

Practical Exercises and Resources

Each chapter of this book includes practical exercises that are designed to help you put what you've learned into action. By working through these exercises, you'll not only solidify your understanding of the branding principles but also start building the foundation for your own standout brand.

Here's what you can expect:

√ **Brand Identity Worksheets**: As you define your brand identity, I've included worksheets to help you clarify your mission, vision, values, and unique selling proposition. These are the cornerstones of your brand, and the exercises will guide you through the process of developing a clear and consistent identity.

√ **Storytelling Prompts**: When we dive into brand storytelling, you'll find specific prompts that help you craft your brand's narrative. These prompts are designed to help you articulate your "why," highlight your customer success stories, and share the journey that led to the creation of your business.

√ **Brand Consistency Checklists**: A key factor in branding is ensuring consistency, but I know that this ensuring consistency across all your branding efforts can be a challenge. In the chapters on brand consistency, you'll find checklists to help you audit your current branding efforts and ensure that your messaging, visuals, and customer interactions are aligned across all channels.

√ **AI and Branding Tools**: When we discuss how to leverage AI to enhance your branding, you'll find a list of tools and software that can help you automate, personalize, and analyze your brand's performance. These resources will help you stay ahead of the curve as AI continues to transform the branding landscape.

These exercises and resources are designed to move you from theory to action, so be sure to take full advantage of them as you work through each chapter.

NEXT STEPS AFTER EACH CHAPTER

Branding is a process, and each chapter builds on the last. At the end of every chapter, you'll find clear next steps to guide you on how to implement what you've learned.

Here's how to approach these next steps:
- √ **Reflect on Key Insights**: Each chapter will challenge you to think about branding in new ways. After you finish reading, take a moment to reflect on how the ideas presented apply to your business. Consider writing down your thoughts and observations, as this will help you stay focused on the areas that need the most attention.
- √ **Complete the Exercises**: Don't skip the exercises! They are essential for putting the concepts into practice. Even if an exercise seems simple, it's designed to give you clarity and actionable insights that will contribute to building a strong brand. Dedicate time to complete these tasks before moving on to the next chapter.
- √ **Track Your Progress**: As you work through the book, keep track of the progress you're making. You may want to use a journal or digital document to record the actions you're taking and the results you're seeing. This will help you stay accountable

and measure the impact of the branding strategies on your business.

√ **Make Adjustments**: Building a brand is an ongoing process. After each chapter, you may realize that certain areas of your branding need to be adjusted or refined. Don't be afraid to revisit earlier chapters and make changes based on new insights. A great brand is always evolving, so flexibility is key.

√ **Engage with the Community**: Branding doesn't happen in isolation. As you implement the strategies in this book, engage with other entrepreneurs, small business owners, and branding professionals. Whether it's through online forums, social media, or networking events, connecting with others will give you new ideas and perspectives that can enhance your branding efforts.

By following these steps after each chapter, you'll not only deepen your understanding of branding but also see tangible improvements in how your business is perceived by your audience. The goal is to equip you with the tools and knowledge to create a brand that stands out and drives long-term success.

CHAPTER 1: BUILDING A BRAND PEOPLE BELIEVE IN – THE BRAND BELIEF SYSTEM

A powerful brand isn't just something people buy; it's something they believe in. A brand that resonates on a deep, personal level goes beyond offering products and services—it becomes a part of people's lives and values. This connection doesn't happen by chance; it's built through intentional strategy and storytelling. In this chapter, we'll explore how to create a brand belief system—a framework of seven essential elements that turn your brand into something your audience believes in, trusts, and feels connected to.

The brand belief system consists of seven primary components, which includes the origin story, purpose, symbols, routines, opponents, language, and visionary. Each element serves a specific role in shaping the identity and perception of your brand. When these elements work together, they create a powerful and cohesive brand that people don't just purchase—they champion. Let's break down each piece of the brand belief system and explore how you can use them to build a strong, lasting brand.

The 7 Key Components of the Brand Belief System

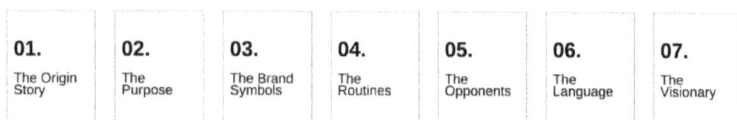

01.	02.	03.	04.	05.	06.	07.
The Origin Story	The Purpose	The Brand Symbols	The Routines	The Opponents	The Language	The Visionary

thisisbrandingbook.com

The Origin Story

Every great brand has an origin story—a narrative about how it started, what challenges it overcame, and the inspiration behind it. The origin story is not just about the facts; it's about creating an emotional connection with your audience. It gives people insight into your brand's journey and helps them relate to the values and motivations that shaped it. A strong origin story humanizes your brand and creates a sense of authenticity. People are drawn to stories because they provide context and meaning. When customers understand where your brand came from, they feel more connected to it. They become part of your journey, not just consumers of your products.

Think about the defining moments that led to the creation of your brand. What problem were you trying to solve? What inspired you to take the leap? Were there any major challenges you had to overcome along the way? These moments form the foundation of your origin story.

For example, **Apple's origin story** is famously tied to Steve Jobs and Steve Wozniak building the first Apple computer in a garage. The story conveys a sense of innovation, determination, and a desire to challenge the status quo. Even decades later, Apple's origin story continues to be a key part of its brand identity, reinforcing the idea that Apple is a brand for creators, thinkers, and innovators.

Tips for Crafting Your Origin Story:
- √ Focus on authenticity—don't embellish or make up elements just for effect.
- √ Highlight the challenges you overcame, as this adds depth and relatability.
- √ Make sure your story ties back to your brand's core mission and values.

The Purpose

Purpose is the "why" behind your brand—why your brand exists beyond making a profit. It's the deeper mission or belief that drives everything you do. Purpose answers questions like, "What impact does your brand want to have on the world?" or "What problem is your brand committed to solving?"

Customers today are looking for brands that align with their personal values and beliefs. A clear and meaningful purpose differentiates your brand and creates loyalty. When people see that your brand stands for something they care about, they're more likely to connect with it on a deeper level and become long-term advocates.

To define your purpose, start by identifying the core values that guide your brand. What do you believe in? What change do you want to make in the world? Your purpose should be specific, actionable, and deeply rooted in your brand's identity.

Example: Apple's purpose has always been centered around innovation, creativity, and empowering individuals. The company's mission to "think different" positioned it as a brand that challenges norms and gives people the tools to create and explore their ideas. This purpose has been a cornerstone of Apple's success, driving everything from product design to marketing campaigns.

Tips for Articulating Your Purpose:
- √ Ensure your purpose is clear and actionable, not vague or generic.
- √ Tie your purpose back to the benefits you deliver to customers.
- √ Your purpose should guide decision-making at every level of your business.

The Symbols
Symbols are the visual elements that represent your brand, from your logo and color scheme to product design and packaging. These symbols serve as shorthand for your brand's identity and evoke an emotional response. The right symbols can make your brand instantly recognizable and memorable.

Symbols are a powerful part of your brand identity because they visually communicate who you are. A well-designed logo or product can trigger immediate recognition and recall, reinforcing the emotional connection between your brand and your audience. Strong symbols help your brand stand out and make a lasting impression.

Your brand's symbols should reflect its values,

personality, and purpose. Start by thinking about what feelings and associations you want to evoke when people see your logo, product packaging, or website. Consistency is key—every visual element should align with your overall brand identity.

Example: Apple's sleek, minimalist product design is one of the most recognizable symbols of the brand. The simplicity of its products—whether it's the iPhone, MacBook, or iPad—reflects Apple's commitment to user-friendly innovation. Apple's iconic logo, a simple apple with a bite taken out, has become a global symbol of creativity and innovation.

Tips for Choosing Your Brand's Symbols:
- √ Simplicity is powerful—don't overcomplicate your logo or visuals.
- √ Ensure your visual elements are consistent across all platforms and products.
- √ Your symbols should align with the emotions you want to evoke in your audience.

The Routines
Routines refer to how your audience interacts with your brand on a regular basis. It's about making your brand a part of their daily lives. This could be through the products they use, the apps they open, or the content they consume.

Brands that become part of their customers' routines are more likely to foster long-term loyalty. When your products or services seamlessly fit into your customers' lives, they become indispensable. The more integrated your brand is into your customers' habits, the harder it is for competitors to replace you.

Think about how your product or service fits into your customers' everyday lives and whether there are ways to make your brand more useful or relevant to their daily routine. This could mean offering convenience, creating a subscription-based service, or designing products that customers rely on regularly.

Example: Apple has mastered the art of integrating its products into people's daily routines. From checking emails on an iPhone in the morning to working on a MacBook throughout the day and unwinding with Apple Music or Apple TV at night, Apple's ecosystem of products fits seamlessly into users' routines. The more products a person uses, the more embedded Apple is in their lives.

Tips for Creating Brand Routines:
- √ Look for ways to make your product or service essential to your customers' daily habits.
- √ Consider offering services that promote repeat use, like subscription models or options that provide add-on convenience.
- √ Encourage regular engagement through reminders, updates, or personalized experiences.

The Opponents – What Your Brand Stands Against
Opponents in branding refer to the values, ideas, or institutions your brand positions itself against. This doesn't necessarily mean attacking competitors, but rather defining what your brand doesn't stand for. This contrast helps clarify your brand's values and gives your audience something to rally behind.

Defining what your brand opposes helps sharpen your identity and attract like-minded customers. It's not just about what you stand for, but what you stand against. Opponents create a sense of urgency and help your brand carve out a unique position in the market.

Consider the norms or behaviors in your industry that you reject. What frustrations do your customers have that your brand is working to eliminate? Identifying what you stand against makes it easier for customers to align with your mission.

Example: From its earliest days, Apple positioned itself as the brand for rebels and non-conformists, standing against the "Big Brother" culture of IBM and other tech giants. The famous "1984" commercial symbolized this, presenting Apple as the choice for creative thinkers who wanted to break free from conformity. This stance against the status quo has been a defining part of Apple's brand ever since.

Tips for Defining Your Opponents:
   √   Avoid making direct attacks on competitors— instead, focus on the values you oppose.
   √   Be specific about what you reject in your industry or market.
   √   Use opponents to sharpen your brand's position and differentiate it from the competition.

The Language
Language refers to the words, phrases, and tone your brand uses to communicate with its audience. From your tagline to your social media posts, the language you use shapes how people perceive your brand. Language is a

critical part of creating a unique voice and reinforcing your brand's identity.

Your brand's language should be consistent and recognizable across all communication channels. The way you speak to your audience should reflect your brand's personality and values. Whether you're playful, professional, or provocative, your language sets the tone for how customers engage with your brand.

Define your brand's personality first, then craft messaging that reflects that identity. Are you authoritative, friendly, or quirky? Your brand's voice should feel natural and authentic, making it easy for customers to understand and connect with.

Example: Apple's language has always been simple, clear, and innovative. Taglines like "Think Different" and product names like "iPhone" or "iPad" are minimalist but profound, capturing the essence of Apple's brand. Their marketing copy reflects this tone as well—straightforward, user-friendly, and focused on empowering customers.

Tips for Crafting Your Brand's Language:
- √ Keep it simple and consistent—your audience should immediately recognize your tone.
- √ Make sure your language reflects your brand's personality.
- √ Use language to convey your core values and message clearly.

The Visionary – Embodying the Brand

The visionary represents the face of your brand—the individual or figure that embodies everything your brand stands for. This could be the founder, a spokesperson, or even a mascot. The visionary's role is to personify the brand's values and purpose, giving customers someone they can relate to and trust.

Having a recognizable leader adds a human element to your brand. The concept that "people buy from people" underscores the importance of **humanizing a brand** by connecting it with a relatable figure who embodies its values, vision, and mission. When positioning your brand with a person at the forefront, particularly with **"the Visionary"**, you leverage the power of human connection to foster trust, inspire loyalty, and create deeper emotional engagement. Customers are more likely to connect with a person than with a company logo or corporate entity. The visionary becomes the storyteller, the champion, and the living example of the brand.

If you're the founder of your business, you're likely the face of the brand. It's important to embody the values, personality, and mission you want your audience to connect with. If you're not the face, choose a spokesperson who represents your brand authentically and consistently.

Example: Steve Jobs was more than just Apple's CEO—he was the heart of the brand. His vision, passion, and focus on innovation defined Apple's identity. Jobs embodied the rebellious, creative spirit of Apple, making him the perfect person to represent the brand's values and connect with its audience on a personal level.

Tips for Defining Your Brand's Visionary:
- √ Choose someone who truly embodies your brand's values.
- √ Be consistent—your leader should represent the brand in a way that aligns with your messaging.
- √ Make sure your visionary is relatable and credible, creating a sense of trust with your audience.

The brand belief system is a powerful framework for building a brand that goes beyond products and services. When you define your origin story, purpose, symbols, routines, opponents, language, and visionary, you create a cohesive and authentic brand that resonates deeply with your audience. Your brand becomes more than a business—it becomes a movement, a lifestyle, and a belief system that customers want to be part of.

By focusing on these seven elements, you can build a brand that people don't just buy—they believe in.

WORKSHEET
CLARIFYING YOUR BRAND BELIEF SYSTEM

To build a powerful brand that resonates with your audience, it's essential to understand the core beliefs that drive your business. Your brand beliefs go beyond the products or services you offer—they reflect the deeper values and purpose behind your brand. Use this worksheet to gain clarity on what your brand stands for and how it connects with your audience on a meaningful level.

Instructions: Reflect on the questions below and write down your responses. These insights will help you articulate your brand's belief system and align your messaging with what matters most to your customers.

Step 1: Understanding Your Brand's Core Values
What do your customers care about?
Think about your target audience. What values, desires, or needs drive their purchasing decisions? What matters most to them when they interact with your brand?

Write your response:

_____

How does your brand add meaning to their lives?
Beyond the products or services you offer, how does your brand positively impact your customers' lives? What emotional or practical benefits do they gain from choosing your brand?

Write your response:

_____

What larger impact does your brand strive to make?
Consider the bigger picture. How does your brand contribute to society, the environment, or a specific cause? What's the purpose beyond profit?

Write your response:

_____

Step 2: Connecting Your Beliefs to Your Products
How does your brand influence the products or services you offer?
Does your brand's belief system shape the way you design, develop, or offer your products or services?
In what ways are your offerings aligned with your core values?

Write your response:

_____

What makes your brand exist in the first place?
Go back to the very reason your business was created. What core belief or need inspired you to start your brand, and how is that reflected in what you offer?

Write your response:

_____

Step 3: Defining What Your Audience Should Believe
What do you want customers to believe about themselves through your brand?

Think about how your brand helps customers see themselves. What transformation do you want them to experience? How do you want them to feel after engaging with your brand?

Write your response:

_____

Step 4: Gathering Outside Perspectives
Ask real customers or friends to describe their experience with your brand.

Reach out to customers or close friends and ask them to share their experiences. What words do they use to describe your brand? How do they feel after interacting with your product or service?

Key insights from customer feedback:

_____

Step 5: Bringing It All Together
Now that you've answered these questions, take a moment to review your responses. Use this clarity to articulate your brand's belief system in a few sentences. These beliefs will help shape your messaging, guide your marketing strategy, and strengthen your connection with your audience.

My Brand's Belief System:

_____

_____

_____

_____

_____

_____

_____

_____

_____

_____

_____

_____

_____

_____

_____

_____

By aligning your brand's actions, messaging, and products with these core beliefs, you'll create a brand that not only resonates with your audience but also stands for something meaningful, fostering loyalty and long-term engagement.

"

Why should you build your brand on beliefs, not benefits or features?

Because in a world where consumers have endless options, a brand that stands for something meaningful will always have the advantage.

thisisbrandingbook.com

CHAPTER 2:
THE MYTHS OF BRANDING

"Every CEO, entrepreneur, and visionary wants their product or service to connect with people—with resonance, emotion, and meaning. People are drawn to brands that are more than just products. They are drawn to brands that tell a story, that represents something bigger than themselves. Brands that people can believe in."

Branding is often misunderstood, especially by entrepreneurs and small business owners who are just starting to navigate the complexities of building a standout business. There are many misconceptions about what branding is and what it can do for a company. These myths can hold you back, prevent you from fully embracing branding, and limit your business's potential for success.

In this chapter, we're going to debunk five of the most common myths about branding before we dive deeper. By understanding the truth behind these misconceptions, you'll be better equipped to make strategic decisions that will strengthen your brand and set you apart from the competition.

The 5 Myths About Branding That Will Change Your Perspective

Branding Is Just a Logo

Branding Is Expensive

Branding Doesn't Impact Sales

Branding Cannot Be Measured

Marketing Is Necessary, but Branding Isn't.

BONUS: Branding is Only for Large Corporations

thisisbrandingbook.com

Debunking Common Branding Misconceptions
Many entrepreneurs believe that branding is a vague, abstract concept that doesn't directly impact their business or their bottom line. The truth is branding is one of the most powerful tools you have to differentiate your business and create long-lasting customer relationships. When done correctly, branding influences everything—

from how your customers perceive you to how they feel about your products or services. Let's take a closer look at the five most common myths that stop businesses from fully embracing branding and the reality behind them.

MYTH 1: BRANDING IS JUST A LOGO
One of the biggest misconceptions about branding is that it begins and ends with your logo. While your logo is an important visual representation of your brand, it's just one piece of a much larger puzzle. Branding encompasses every aspect of how your business is perceived by your audience. It's about the emotions and experiences your business evokes, the story you tell, and the promise you deliver to your customers.

Your logo is a visual symbol of your brand identity, but it's not the entirety of your brand. Think of your logo as the tip of the iceberg. The real substance of your brand lies beneath the surface—in your mission, values, messaging, and how you connect with your audience on an emotional level.

For example, think about brands like Nike or Apple. Yes, their logos are instantly recognizable, but what really makes those brands powerful are the feelings they evoke—empowerment, innovation, and simplicity. Their branding goes beyond the logo to create a lasting emotional connection with their customers.

The Reality: Branding is the sum of every interaction a customer has with a company. It is your company's values, messaging, visuals, and customer interactions. It includes your tone of voice, customer service, company values, and even the way you respond to feedback. The emotional and psychological connection your audience has with your business, or your logo is just one part of that experience. A strong brand creates a cohesive and memorable experience across all touchpoints.

This is Branding Example: Airbnb

Between 2020 and 2024, Airbnb has solidified itself as one of the most recognizable brands in the travel industry, but not just because of its logo. The company's brand is built on the idea of "belonging anywhere" and fostering connections between hosts and travelers.

During the pandemic, when travel was severely impacted, Airbnb adapted its brand messaging to focus on local and safe travel experiences, such as their **"Live Anywhere"** campaign in 2021. This pivot highlighted how branding goes beyond a logo—it's about crafting meaningful messages and experiences that resonate with the times. The brand's success wasn't driven by its logo but by its adaptability and emphasis on community.

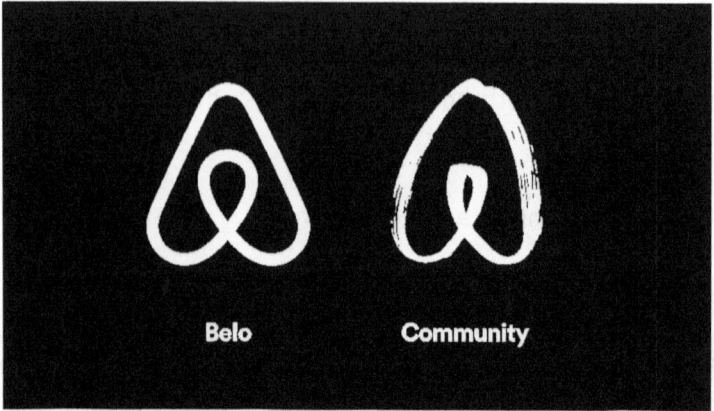

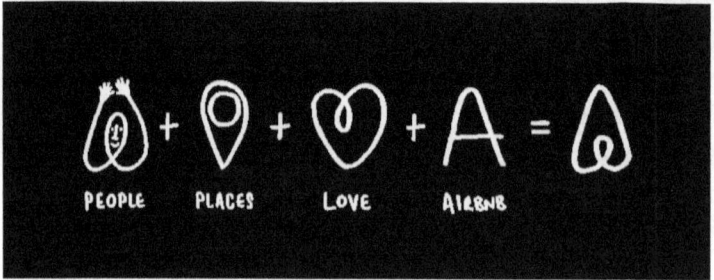

The bélo stands for four things: people, places, love and airbnb.

CASE STUDY

Airbnb's journey from its modest beginnings in 2008 to becoming a global leader in the travel and hospitality sector is a testament to the power of branding, marketing, and design. What started with the simple idea of renting out air mattresses in a San Francisco apartment has grown into a platform with millions of listings across more than 200 countries. This case study examines Airbnb's early challenges, the innovative strategies they employed, and the key factors that contributed to their success.

Gaining Traction with Limited Resources

In its early stages, Airbnb struggled to gain users, facing an uphill battle with limited resources and no brand recognition. The founders initially turned to their personal networks, asking friends, family, and acquaintances to try the platform. However, to scale, they needed more creative solutions to attract both hosts and guests. This is where guerrilla marketing tactics came into play, like the 2008 Democratic National Convention, where Airbnb distributed branded cereal boxes to generate buzz and media attention.

Breakthrough in Digital Marketing
1. SEO & Content Marketing

Airbnb's first major success came through its focus on **Search Engine Optimization (SEO)** and content marketing. The company quickly recognized the importance of ranking highly on search engines for vacation rental-related terms. By optimizing their website and producing city guides and neighborhood reviews, Airbnb successfully positioned itself as a go-to source for travel information. This not only increased their organic traffic but also enhanced their credibility and brand recognition.

2. Email Marketing

Personalized email marketing was another pivotal tool in Airbnb's strategy. The company sent tailored emails that were carefully segmented and featuring new listings, promotions, and local events to engage users. They also implemented referral programs, encouraging users to invite friends and family to join, which greatly expanded their reach. The power of word-of-mouth, amplified by digital referrals, helped the company grow at an exponential rate.

3. Social Media Marketing

Social media became a cornerstone of Airbnb's marketing and branding strategy, leveraging platforms like Instagram, Facebook, Twitter, and Pinterest.

- √ On **Instagram**, Airbnb shared visually stunning photos of unique properties and destinations, prompting users to engage with the brand and share their own travel experiences.
- √ **Facebook** ads allowed for precise targeting, helping Airbnb reach specific audiences with tailored campaigns.
- √ On **Twitter (now X)**, they ran creative campaigns like #LiveInTheMovies, encouraging users to share their favorite movie locations for a chance to stay in similar homes. Connecting travel emotions to an aspirational lifestyle.
- √ On **Pinterest**, Airbnb curated travel inspiration and home décor ideas, tapping into users' wanderlust and desire for unique experiences.
- √ This multi-platform strategy not only grew brand awareness but also fostered a global community.

Advertising Evolution: Early Focus on Online Channels
Airbnb's initial advertising efforts relied heavily on **Google AdWords** and **Facebook Ads**, enabling them to reach targeted demographics and scale effectively with limited resources. With Google processing billions of searches each day, Airbnb capitalized on keywords related to travel and accommodations to drive substantial traffic to their platform.

Expansion into Traditional Media
As Airbnb expanded, they ventured into traditional advertising channels like print, radio, and television. Their 2014 **"Belong Anywhere"** campaign featured real host and guest stories, illustrating the unique experiences made possible through Airbnb further expanding their brand messaging. This marked their transition from being a niche platform to becoming a household name.

Experiential Marketing
In addition to traditional and digital advertising, Airbnb embraced **experiential marketing** by hosting events and pop-ups. One notable example was the **Airbnb Park at the 2013 Sundance Film Festival**, where unique accommodations were showcased, allowing users to engage with the brand in a tangible, memorable way.

Design Overhaul: Crafting a Visual Identity
Initial Design Challenges
In its early days, Airbnb's design lacked cohesion. The original website was cluttered, and user-generated photos were of poor quality, which hurt user trust. This changed when co-founder Joe Gebbia noticed a trend: poor-quality photos were affecting bookings. By personally taking high-quality images of listings, Airbnb saw profits double in just one week, proving that design and visuals were critical to the platform's success.

Rebranding with the Bélo
Airbnb's 2014 rebranding project with the **Bélo** that was led by London-based **DesignStudio**, was a game-changer. The new **Bélo** logo—a heart, a location pin, and the letter "A"—symbolized a sense of belonging and

connection, resonating deeply with the platform's mission. This rebranding extended beyond the logo, encompassing typography, color palettes, and a cohesive visual identity that united all touchpoints of the brand.

Despite initial criticism, the rebrand ultimately helped solidify Airbnb's position in the travel market, creating a recognizable and emotionally resonant brand image.

User Experience Innovations

Airbnb's commitment to continuous **User Experience (UX) improvements** played a significant role in their success. Over time, they streamlined the booking process, introduced instant booking, personalized recommendations, and an in-app messaging feature. These updates enhanced usability and made the platform more intuitive for both hosts and guests, improving trust and satisfaction across the board.

A Roadmap to Success

Airbnb's transformation from a fledgling startup to a global giant was built on a foundation of smart marketing, innovative design, and a relentless focus on user experience. From the strategic use of digital marketing and SEO to the creation of an inclusive brand identity with the Bélo, Airbnb's success offers a powerful case study in how to build and scale a brand.

Their success story illustrates the importance of adaptability, creativity, and a customer-centric approach—principles that any brand can apply to grow and thrive in today's competitive marketplace. Airbnb's rise proves that with the right strategies, even the smallest startups can achieve global recognition and success. Their journey offers invaluable lessons for businesses looking to expand their brand reach, enhance customer experience, and leave a lasting impact.

MYTH 2: BRANDING IS EXPENSIVE

Many small business owners believe that branding is something only large corporations can afford. The idea that branding requires a huge budget, fancy marketing agencies, and expensive campaigns is a common but incorrect assumption.

While it's true that big companies can spend millions on branding efforts, you don't need a massive budget to build a strong brand. In fact, some of the most successful brands started with limited resources but made smart, consistent branding decisions. The key to great branding is not how much you spend but how clear, authentic, and consistent your message is.

You can build an impactful brand by focusing on your core values, telling your unique story, and ensuring that your visual identity is cohesive across all platforms. Tools like Canva for designing brand assets, or social media platforms for free marketing, allow even the smallest businesses to create a professional, recognizable brand.

The Reality: Effective branding doesn't require a large budget; it requires clarity and consistency. You don't need an expensive marketing firm to develop a strong brand. Startups and small businesses can successfully build their brand by focusing on authenticity, delivering exceptional customer experiences, and using digital tools to create consistent messaging. What matters most is the clarity and consistency of your message, visuals, and the emotional connection you create with your audience.

This is Branding Example: Gymshark

Founded in 2012, Gymshark started as a small online retailer selling fitness apparel. By 2020, Gymshark had grown into a billion-dollar brand without the kind of high-budget marketing you might expect from such rapid success. The company focused on building its brand by using social media influencers, creating a community of fitness enthusiasts, and engaging with customers directly.

Gymshark's branding was built on authenticity, customer engagement, and a strong online presence—none of which required excessive spending. Their rise proves that building a brand can be affordable, especially in the digital age.

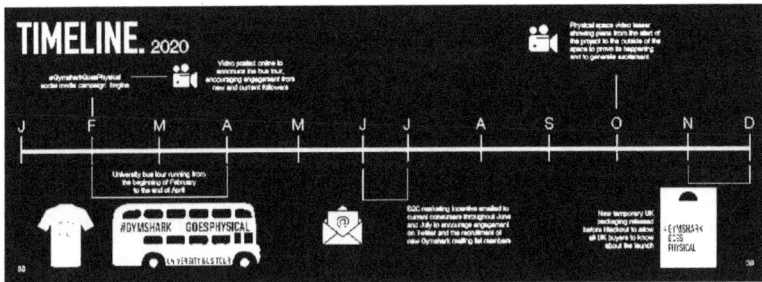

TIMELINE. 2020

J F M A M J J A S O N D

#GYMSHARK GOESPHYSICAL

UNIVERSITY BUS TOUR

Case Study: Gymshark's Rise to Fitness Apparel Leadership Through Strategic Marketing

Gymshark's Journey to Global Success

Gymshark, a fitness apparel brand launched in 2012, has experienced remarkable growth in recent years. With its strategic marketing approach, Gymshark has transformed into one of the most popular names in the fitness industry, capturing the attention of millions of fitness enthusiasts globally.

This case study explores the key components of Gymshark's brand strategy and the marketing techniques that have fueled its rapid ascent.

Building a Strong Brand Identity

A core element of Gymshark's success lies in its powerful brand identity, which deeply resonates with its target audience of young fitness enthusiasts. The brand's messaging revolves around the values of **empowerment**, **authenticity**, and **inclusivity**, positioning Gymshark as more than just an apparel company—it is a lifestyle brand.

From the outset, Gymshark has committed to showcasing real people with diverse body types and fitness levels in its campaigns. This authenticity has allowed the brand to create a relatable image that encourages consumers to see themselves in Gymshark's products. By focusing on relatable role models and real-life fitness journeys, Gymshark has cultivated a loyal following.

Gymshark's dedication to high-quality, performance-driven products further strengthens its brand image. By combining functional design with stylish aesthetics, Gymshark has positioned itself as the go-to brand for fitness enthusiasts who want to look good while achieving their fitness goals. This blend of quality and community has played a crucial role in the brand's ability to stand out in a crowded market.

The Power of Social Media Marketing
Gymshark's social media presence has been central to its marketing strategy and growth. With over 5 million Instagram followers and a significant presence on platforms like YouTube and TikTok, Gymshark has built a direct connection with its audience.

Gymshark's approach to social media goes beyond simply posting product images. The brand excels at creating **engaging and relatable content**, often leveraging customer stories, motivational fitness journeys, and behind-the-scenes content. Through social media, Gymshark has successfully fostered a sense of community and belonging among its audience.

Gymshark also uses social platforms to launch new products, generating excitement with sneak peeks and teasers. This strategy not only builds anticipation but also increases customer engagement before a product release, ensuring successful launches and sellouts.

Influencer Marketing: A Key to Rapid Growth

Influencer marketing has been a crucial factor in Gymshark's rise. The brand has strategically partnered with fitness influencers who embody its values and connect with its target audience. These collaborations have amplified Gymshark's reach, allowing it to tap into the influencers' loyal followings.

One standout example is Gymshark's partnership with fitness influencer **Whitney Simmons**, whose energetic personality and fitness dedication aligned perfectly with Gymshark's ethos. Featuring Simmons in promotional campaigns only strengthened the brand's credibility and provided real-life validation of the products.

These influencer collaborations are not limited to endorsements. Influencers often participate in workout videos, share their fitness routines, and wear Gymshark products in their daily lives. This integration of influencers into Gymshark's storytelling has helped humanize the brand and make it more approachable.

Harnessing User-Generated Content (UGC)

Gymshark has successfully been able to turn its customers into brand advocates by encouraging user-generated content (UGC). Gymshark invites its audience to share their fitness journeys on social media, tagging the brand and using dedicated hashtags to showcase how Gymshark products support their workouts.

By featuring UGC on its official platforms, Gymshark not only validates customer experiences but also enhances brand trust. Customers see real people achieving their goals while using Gymshark apparel, creating a powerful sense of relatability and motivation. This strategy has fostered a close-knit community where customers feel heard and valued, further strengthening their loyalty.

Creating Hype with Innovative Product Launches
Gymshark has mastered the art of building anticipation and demand for new product releases. Before launching a new line, the brand employs **teasers and sneak peeks** to create buzz among its followers. These previews, shared via social media and email, keep Gymshark's audience eagerly awaiting each new drop.

This strategy often includes influencer collaborations, where Gymshark partners with fitness personalities to showcase the upcoming collections. By tapping into influencers' networks, Gymshark can amplify its marketing efforts, drawing attention to new releases from diverse audience segments.

One of Gymshark's most effective tactics has been its **limited-edition releases**, which tap into the psychological principle of scarcity. By offering exclusive, limited-quantity products, Gymshark creates a sense of urgency, driving customers to act quickly. These products, often tied to special collaborations or events, tend to sell out fast, increasing demand and reinforcing the brand's reputation as a trendsetter in fitness fashion.

Community Building: A Foundation for Loyalty

Gymshark has taken its engagement with fitness enthusiasts to the next level by actively building a community around the brand. The company regularly interacts with its customers on social media, responding to comments, answering questions, and showcasing customer success stories. This direct communication helps Gymshark strengthen relationships and build loyalty.

Beyond social media, Gymshark participates in fitness events and organizes meetups for its community members. By sponsoring fitness expos, supporting influencers, and creating unique fitness challenges, Gymshark keeps its audience engaged both online and offline. This approach helps Gymshark stay relevant and connected to its community while encouraging word-of-mouth marketing.

Results: Revenue Growth and Market Expansion

Gymshark's strategic focus on branding, influencer partnerships, and community engagement has led to impressive revenue growth and market share expansion. By maintaining a deep connection with its audience and consistently delivering high-quality products, Gymshark has developed a loyal customer base that continues to drive sales year after year.

The brand's commitment to innovation, both in terms of marketing and product offerings, has positioned Gymshark as a formidable player in the global fitness apparel industry. Its ability to adapt to changing consumer preferences and trends ensures that Gymshark will remain a key player in the industry for years to come.

The Gymshark Blueprint for Success
Gymshark's marketing strategy offers a masterclass in how to build a brand from the ground up through a combination of **authenticity, community engagement**, and **innovative digital marketing**. By leveraging the power of social media, influencers, and user-generated content, Gymshark has created a loyal following and established itself as a trendsetter in the fitness world.

The brand's focus on creating high-quality, performance-driven apparel, while fostering a strong sense of community, has differentiated Gymshark from its competitors and solidified its status as a leader in the fitness apparel industry. Gymshark's marketing success story demonstrates the impact of a well-executed, customer-centric strategy in driving long-term growth.

MYTH 3: BRANDING DOESN'T IMPACT SALES
This myth assumes that branding is a "nice to have" rather than a driver of revenue. However, branding plays a critical role in influencing purchasing decisions and building customer loyalty. A common misconception among businesses, especially startups, is that branding is secondary to sales and revenue generation. This myth suggests that branding is "fluff"—a luxury that can be addressed later, after the business is generating consistent sales. The assumption is that if a product or service is strong enough, sales will follow, and branding is simply a cosmetic layer that can wait.

However, this belief overlooks the critical role branding plays in **driving sales**, building customer loyalty, and differentiating a business in competitive markets. In reality, branding is not a "nice to have"; it's a powerful force that directly influences purchasing decisions, customer retention, and even consumer pricing.

The Reality: Branding Fuels Sales Growth
Branding is not just about visuals or marketing gimmicks; it's about creating a meaningful identity that resonates with customers. A strong brand fosters **trust, recognition, and emotional connection**, all of which are key drivers of sales. In markets where many businesses offer similar products or services, branding becomes the primary differentiator that can capture attention and inspire loyalty.

Customers don't just buy products—they buy into **brands** they trust and feel connected to. Branding provides an emotional anchor that leads to higher customer retention, repeat business, and often allows businesses to charge premium prices. This emotional connection is what turns one-time buyers into loyal customers, creating long-term value that goes beyond a single transaction.

This is Branding Example: Patagonia

Patagonia, a high-end outdoor apparel company, has become a standout brand not just for its durable clothing, but for its strong commitment to environmental sustainability. The company has taken an unconventional approach to marketing, actively promoting the idea of **buying less** and encouraging the purchase of used goods instead of new products.

Despite what might seem like a counterintuitive strategy, Patagonia has seen its revenues grow, even as many traditional retailers have struggled. How did Patagonia manage to turn this seemingly anti-sales message into a booming business?

DON'T BUY THIS JACKET

"Don't Buy This Jacket" Campaign
During the aftermath of the Great Recession, consumer behavior shifted. People became more cautious with their spending, focusing on value and durability rather than impulse buying. Patagonia recognized this shift and saw an opportunity to highlight the longevity and quality of its products. In 2011, the company launched an ad campaign with the headline **"Don't Buy This Jacket"** during the high-traffic Thanksgiving shopping season.

The ad highlighted the environmental cost of producing one of its best-selling fleece jackets and encouraged customers to think twice before purchasing. Rather than pushing consumers to buy new products, Patagonia urged them to consider opting for second-hand items or repairing existing gear.

Key Insights from Patagonia's Strategy:
Focus on Sustainability: Patagonia has built its brand around environmentally responsible practices, which aligns with the values of its target audience.
- √ **Product Durability**: By promoting long-lasting products, Patagonia appeals to customers looking for value over volume.
- √ **Re-commerce Initiatives**: Patagonia has embraced the resale of used goods, creating a circular economy around its products.

Despite urging consumers to rethink their purchases, Patagonia saw a significant increase in sales. Revenues grew by **30% in 2012**, reaching $543 million, with an additional 5% growth in 2013. By 2017, Patagonia's annual sales hit **$1 billion**.

Authenticity in Action
Patagonia's success isn't just about what it says—it's about what it does. Founder **Yvon Chouinard**, a passionate environmentalist and accomplished climber, has made sure that the company's commitment to sustainability goes beyond marketing rhetoric. Patagonia donates a percentage of its revenue to environmental causes and uses recycled materials, organic fabrics, and **Fair-Trade Certified** manufacturing practices in its production process.

In addition to creating sustainable products, Patagonia has implemented several innovative programs. The company launched an **environmentally friendly repair truck** that traveled across the U.S., helping customers repair their worn gear and encouraging them to buy used Patagonia products. Patagonia also invested in **Yerdle**, a startup aimed at reducing unnecessary consumption by promoting the resale of used goods.

In 2017, Patagonia introduced a program offering **store credits** for gently used Patagonia products, which are then cleaned, repaired, and resold through the company's **Worn Wear** initiative. This effort to promote second-hand goods further strengthens the brand's commitment to extending the life cycle of its products and reducing waste.

Aligning with the Right Audience

Patagonia's message resonates deeply with its environmentally conscious target market. These customers are drawn to the brand not just for its high-quality, long-lasting products but for its commitment to ethical business practices. By positioning itself as a company that stands for more than just profit, Patagonia has created a strong bond with consumers who want their purchases to reflect their personal values.

The brand's core audience appreciates Patagonia's efforts to reduce environmental impact through recycling and sustainability, but the appeal goes even further. Some customers, attracted by the brand's **trendiness**, may not prioritize sustainability as much but still buy Patagonia products because of their perceived status and quality.

Additionally, Patagonia's activism speaks to this customer base. In 2018, the company made headlines by donating the **$10 million** it saved from President Trump's 2017 tax cuts to environmental causes, reinforcing its commitment to protecting the planet and finding solutions to the climate crisis. This move further solidified Patagonia's standing as a brand that **walks the talk**.

Patagonia: A Profitable Brand with Purpose
Patagonia has managed to do what few brands can—merge profitability with purpose. By embracing a business model that is at odds with the planned obsolescence strategy of many modern manufacturers, Patagonia has proven that longevity and sustainability can drive growth. Its decision to market used products, promote durability, and limit unnecessary consumption has enhanced its appeal, attracting more customers who view their purchases as a reflection of their personal values.

Through its environmentally focused actions, Patagonia has built an ecosystem around its brand that goes beyond selling products. Its strategy has created a cult-like following of loyal customers who believe in the company's mission to reduce waste and protect the environment. Patagonia's combination of authenticity, activism, and high-quality products has allowed the company to reach over 70 stores worldwide and even venture into the sustainable food business, further expanding its brand reach.

Patagonia's success demonstrates that a brand built on **values** can achieve significant financial growth. By sticking to its principles and creating meaningful connections with its target audience, Patagonia has transformed from a clothing company into a symbol of sustainability and social responsibility. As a result, Patagonia not only continues to thrive in a competitive market but also inspires a new generation of consumers to consider the broader impact of their purchases.

MYTH 4: BRANDING CANNOT BE MEASURED

Measuring the Impact of Branding can seem quite elusive. Many business owners mistakenly believe that branding is too abstract to measure or evaluate. They may assume that because branding focuses on perceptions, emotions, and customer relationships, it's impossible to quantify or determine its effectiveness. This misunderstanding often leads to underestimating the power of branding and its role in driving business success.

In reality, branding is not only measurable but also critical to business growth. There are several **key performance indicators (KPIs)** that can provide concrete insights into how your branding efforts are working. These KPIs allow you to evaluate the success of your brand's identity, message, and positioning, offering a clear picture of how customers perceive and engage with your brand.

Key Branding Metrics to Measure Success
1. Brand Awareness

Brand awareness measures **how well-known** your brand is among your target audience. It's the foundation of a successful brand, as people can't buy from you if they don't know you exist. High brand awareness means your brand is top of mind for consumers when they think about products or services in your industry. This can be tracked through:

√ **Surveys and polls**: Asking your target audience how familiar they are with your brand.

√ **Social media mentions**: Tracking how often people talk about or tag your brand online.

√ **Search volume data**: Monitoring how frequently people are searching for your brand name in Google or other search engines.

Example: If your brand is consistently mentioned on social media or your website traffic spikes due to branded searches, it's a sign that your brand awareness is growing.

2. Customer Loyalty

Customer loyalty looks at **how often customers return** to your business and their likelihood to recommend your brand to others. Strong customer loyalty indicates that your branding resonates with people on a deeper level, building trust and emotional connections that keep them coming back. This metric can be measured by:

√ **Repeat purchase rate**: The percentage of customers who have made multiple purchases from your brand.

√ **Customer lifetime value (CLV)**: How much revenue a customer brings over their entire relationship with your brand.

√ **Net Promoter Score (NPS)**: A customer's likelihood to recommend your brand to others, which reflects their overall satisfaction and loyalty.

Example: A high NPS score or consistent repeat purchases from the same customers demonstrates that your brand has cultivated strong loyalty and advocacy.

3. Engagement Rates

Engagement rates measure **how well your audience is interacting** with your brand across different platforms. Whether it's through social media, email campaigns, or website interactions, high engagement is a clear sign that your brand is capturing attention and fostering meaningful connections. Ways to track engagement include:

- √ **Social media metrics**: Likes, shares, comments, and followers across platforms like Instagram, Facebook, and Twitter.
- √ **Email open and click-through rates**: How often customers open your emails and click on links, showing interest in your messaging and content.
- √ **Website traffic and time spent**: Monitoring how many visitors come to your website, how long they stay, and what they engage with.

  Example: If your social media posts regularly spark conversations or your email campaigns drive high engagement, it's a sign that your branding efforts are connecting with your audience.

4. Brand Sentiment

Brand sentiment reflects **how people feel** about your brand—whether their perception of you is positive, negative, or neutral. This metric goes beyond just numbers and digs into the emotional connection consumers have with your brand. It can be assessed through:

- √ **Customer reviews and testimonials**: Monitoring feedback on platforms like Google Reviews, Yelp, or product pages.
- √ **Surveys**: Asking customers directly about their opinions and feelings toward your brand.

√ **Social listening tools**: Analyzing social media conversations to understand how people talk about your brand, often using sentiment analysis to gauge overall emotion.
Example: If the majority of your customer feedback is positive or if social media sentiment analysis shows an overwhelmingly favorable view of your brand, your branding strategy is hitting the mark.

How These Metrics Impact Your Business

By tracking and analyzing these KPIs, you gain valuable insights into how your brand is performing in the marketplace. These metrics not only show you **what's working** but also help you identify areas where your branding might need improvement. For example:

√ **Increased brand awareness** can lead to greater market share, as more potential customers become familiar with and consider your brand.

√ **High customer loyalty** means your business benefits from repeat sales and word-of-mouth recommendations, reducing the need for constant customer acquisition efforts.

√ **Strong engagement rates** indicate that your brand is resonating with your audience, encouraging them to interact with your content and potentially leading to conversions.

√ **Positive brand sentiment** reflects a strong emotional connection with your audience, which can be the difference between a one-time purchase and a lifelong customer relationship.

The Reality: Branding is Quantifiable and Actionable
Far from being too intangible to measure, branding can and should be **regularly evaluated** using these KPIs. By understanding how brand awareness, customer loyalty, engagement, and sentiment affect your business, you can make data-driven decisions to strengthen your brand's presence in the market.

Branding is not just about how you look or what you say—it's about how people **experience** and **remember** you, and these metrics provide the tools to ensure your branding efforts are aligned with your business goals.

This is Branding Example: Peloton

Peloton, the popular fitness brand that offers high-tech exercise bikes, treadmills, and an immersive fitness experience, has shown that **branding can indeed be measured**. Far from just selling exercise equipment, Peloton has built an entire **ecosystem of fitness enthusiasts** who view their fitness journey as part of a larger, supportive community. Through smart branding and effective marketing campaigns, Peloton has managed to capture the hearts and minds of its users, with measurable outcomes that demonstrate the power of brand loyalty, engagement, and retention.

Below we'll explore how Peloton's branding success defies the myth that branding cannot be measured by providing specific metrics and highlighting the impact of their marketing efforts.

Peloton's brand revolves around more than just the functionality of its equipment. The company has built its brand on the principles of **personal transformation, community, and motivation**. Its users don't just buy a bike or treadmill—they join a global fitness movement. Peloton's success lies in how it has fostered a deeply emotional connection with its audience, and this connection can be quantified through a range of metrics.

KPI's for Measuring Peloton's Branding Success: Customer Engagement
- √ **App Usage**: Peloton's app, which offers live and on-demand classes, has been a core driver of engagement. In 2021 alone, Peloton members completed over **134 million workouts**, a significant increase from the previous year. This

massive level of engagement highlights how users are not just passively interacting with the brand but are deeply invested in it.

√ **Class Participation**: During 2020 and 2021, the average number of workouts per month per Peloton user increased to **21 workouts per month**, compared to just 12 the year prior. This indicates that Peloton has successfully engaged its users and kept them coming back for more.

Customer Retention and Loyalty

Subscriber Retention Rate: One of the most important metrics for measuring brand success is retention. Peloton boasts an impressive **12-month retention rate of 92%** for its connected fitness subscribers as of 2021, demonstrating that once customers engage with the brand, they remain loyal. This retention is a clear indicator that Peloton's brand goes beyond a one-time purchase—it fosters long-term relationships.

Membership Growth: In 2020, Peloton's total membership base grew to **5.9 million members**, up from 1.4 million in 2019. This rapid growth can be attributed to the brand's ability to create a community that members want to be a part of, especially during the COVID pandemic helping Peloton retain its users over time.

Social Media Engagement

Hashtag Campaigns: One of the defining aspects of Peloton's community-building strategy has been its social media engagement. Like its hashtag campaigns *#TogetherWeGoFar*. This campaign helped bring users together during the height of the COVID-19 pandemic, encouraging them to share their workout journeys, motivating each other to stay active.

User-Generated Content: Peloton has a highly engaged social media following, with over **2 million Instagram followers** and tens of thousands of posts using Peloton-related hashtags. This user-generated content further strengthens Peloton's brand by showcasing real stories of transformation and community, which in turn boosts brand awareness and loyalty.

Brand Sentiment and Emotional Connection

Net Promoter Score (NPS): Peloton's NPS, which measures customer loyalty and the likelihood of users recommending the brand to others, is remarkably high, hovering between **80-90**. This score is a clear indicator of the positive emotional connection customers feel toward the brand.

Testimonials and Reviews: Peloton users frequently share their personal transformation stories on social media and in product reviews. From physical health improvements to mental well-being, these stories demonstrate the deep emotional bond users form with the brand, contributing to high levels of brand sentiment.

Branding That Demonstrates Measurable Success

Peloton's marketing and branding campaigns have been pivotal in creating a strong and measurable connection with its audience. These campaigns have not only driven growth in sales but have also enhanced customer engagement, retention, and loyalty.

1. "More Than a Bike" Campaign (2021)

In 2021, Peloton launched its **"More Than a Bike"** campaign to emphasize that Peloton is not just a piece of exercise equipment but a comprehensive fitness experience. The campaign highlighted the **community aspect** of Peloton, showing how users connect with each other and with instructors, and the mental and physical benefits of joining the Peloton community.

Impact: Following the launch of this campaign, Peloton saw an increase in new subscriptions and higher engagement rates among current users. By positioning itself as a lifestyle and community brand rather than a product brand, Peloton was able to enhance its emotional appeal, driving **new subscriber growth** while reinforcing loyalty among existing members.

2. "We All Have Our Reasons" Campaign (2022)

Peloton's **"We All Have Our Reasons"** campaign focused on user-generated content, showcasing the personal motivations of different Peloton members. The campaign featured real stories from Peloton users, highlighting why they ride, run, or meditate with Peloton and how it has positively impacted their lives.

Impact: The campaign led to an increase in both social media engagement and brand sentiment. User participation in social media challenges surged, and the emotional resonance of the campaign helped further solidify Peloton's status as a brand that truly understands and connects with its community.

3. Global Expansion and Localization (2022-2024)

Peloton expanded into **international markets** like Germany and Australia, carefully tailoring its branding to fit local cultures while maintaining its core identity. Through local marketing campaigns and partnerships with regional influencers, Peloton strengthened its global presence.

Impact: By 2023, Peloton's international subscriber base grew by 50%, showing how well the brand could resonate with new audiences. The success of its localized branding strategies proved that Peloton's emotional connection could be replicated across different cultural contexts.

Peloton's branding strategy proves that the impact of branding can be measured in multiple, meaningful ways. Through metrics like **engagement rates, customer retention, social media interaction, and brand sentiment**, Peloton has demonstrated the tangible value of a strong brand.

By focusing on building a community around personal transformation, motivation, and connection, Peloton has managed to turn its brand into a global fitness phenomenon with **measurable success**.

Peloton's ability to create long-lasting emotional connections with users has driven exponential growth in membership, engagement, and customer loyalty, further showcasing that branding is not only powerful—it's measurable and essential for long-term business success.

MYTH 5: MARKETING IS NECESSARY, BUT BRANDING ISN'T.

A common misconception among entrepreneurs and small business owners is that **marketing alone is enough** to drive success. They often pour their energy and budget into ads, promotions, and lead generation, believing these efforts will lead to sustainable growth. The assumption is that if you can drive enough traffic, attract enough eyeballs, or generate enough leads, the business will thrive. This leads many to downplay or neglect the importance of branding.

While marketing is indeed critical for **generating awareness** and **attracting customers**, it's branding that builds **long-term value**, customer loyalty, and a **recognizable identity** in the market. Marketing may bring customers to your door, but without a strong brand, those customers are unlikely to return. **Marketing sells your product; branding sells your business.**

The Reality: Branding Fuels Long-Term Success

Branding and marketing work in tandem, but they serve different purposes. **Marketing** is about promoting your products or services and driving immediate results. It's designed to capture attention, drive traffic, and create conversions. In contrast, **branding** is about shaping perceptions, building trust, and creating a lasting emotional connection between your business and your customers.

Here's the key distinction: **marketing creates short-term gains**, but **branding creates long-term loyalty**. Without branding, your marketing efforts may be effective at bringing in one-time buyers, but they won't foster the emotional engagement that keeps customers coming back. **Branding gives your marketing context, meaning, and continuity.**

BRANDING MATTERS AS MUCH AS MARKETING
Branding Builds Trust and Credibility
Marketing can grab attention, but branding builds trust. When customers see consistent messaging, visuals, and values from your business, it reinforces your credibility and reliability. A strong brand reassures customers that they can trust your company to deliver on its promises, and this trust is what ultimately converts first-time buyers into loyal, repeat customers.

Branding Drives Customer Loyalty and Advocacy
Marketing can generate sales, but it's branding that creates a **community of loyal customers**. A strong brand shapes how customers feel about your business, and those positive feelings foster loyalty. Customers are more likely to return to a brand they feel emotionally connected to. Moreover, loyal customers become brand advocates, spreading the word and helping your business grow organically.

Branding Ensures Consistency in Marketing
Without clear branding, your marketing messages can feel inconsistent, fragmented, or less impactful. A brand provides the **framework** that guides all your marketing efforts, ensuring that every ad, social media post, and piece of content reflects your company's values and identity. When branding and marketing align, the result is a powerful, cohesive message that strengthens your presence in the marketplace.

Branding Allows You to Charge Premium Prices

Marketing can generate sales, but it's branding that allows you to **command premium prices**. When customers perceive a brand as valuable, they're willing to pay more for the products and services it offers. Branding shifts the focus from competing on price to competing on value, allowing you to differentiate your business in a crowded market.

The Power of Branding and Marketing Together

Ultimately, branding and marketing are **two sides of the same coin**. Marketing generates leads, boosts sales, and attracts attention, while branding builds a foundation of trust, loyalty, and emotional connection that ensures customers remember and return to your business.

Here's how branding amplifies marketing efforts:

√ **Brand Awareness**: Marketing campaigns, from digital ads to influencer partnerships, raise awareness about your product or service, but branding ensures that people remember your company in the long term. When your brand is well-defined, marketing efforts have a stronger impact because people can easily associate your promotions with a brand they recognize and trust.

√ **Customer Retention**: Marketing may secure the first sale, but branding keeps customers coming back. Retention is more cost-effective than acquisition, and branding helps ensure that your customers stay loyal to your business.

√ **Brand Differentiation**: In saturated markets, branding is what sets your business apart. Your marketing messages will be more effective if they're anchored in a clear, differentiated brand identity that resonates with your audience.

The myth that "marketing is necessary, but branding isn't" couldn't be further from the truth. **Marketing drives immediate results**, but **branding creates long-term success**. Together, they form a powerful combination that ensures your business not only attracts customers but keeps them loyal over time.

To grow a successful business, you need to do more than just market your products or services—you need to **build a brand that resonates**, creates lasting emotional connections, and provides a clear sense of identity. When marketing and branding work hand in hand, your business is set up for both short-term gains and long-term growth.

This is Branding Example: Chipotle

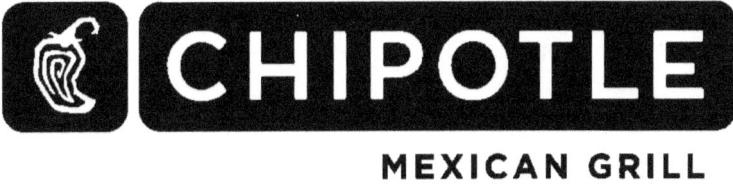

Chipotle Mexican Grill, a leader in the fast-casual restaurant space, provides a powerful case study of how branding is not only necessary but also crucial for sustained growth and recovery. By aligning its brand around the concept of **"food with integrity"**, Chipotle has shown that a strong brand identity does far more than support marketing efforts—it builds **trust, loyalty, and long-term success**. This case study explores how Chipotle's branding defies the myth that "Branding Isn't

Necessary, but Marketing Is," highlighting the specific details and campaigns that prove branding is essential for business growth.

REAL INGREDIENTS. REAL PURPOSE. REAL FLAVOR.

Chipotle's Shift to "Food with Integrity"

After experiencing a series of food safety crises in 2015 and 2016, Chipotle faced significant reputational damage, with sales plummeting by **30% in 2016**. This challenging period highlighted the need for more than just tactical marketing efforts; it required a **rebrand** that would rebuild trust with customers and refocus the company around its core values.

In response, Chipotle leaned into its **"food with integrity"** brand promise, emphasizing sustainability, transparency, and ethical sourcing. Rather than merely launching marketing campaigns to regain customers, Chipotle doubled down on **defining its brand identity**—centered on serving fresh, responsibly sourced ingredients. This rebranding effort wasn't just about selling burritos; it was about telling the story behind the food and reaffirming Chipotle's commitment to quality.

The Power of Branding: Chipotle's Core Strategy

Chipotle's success in the years following its rebrand proves that branding is much more than an afterthought.

By rebuilding its brand around values that resonate with modern consumers, Chipotle reinforced its **core identity**, allowing marketing to amplify that message more effectively. This alignment between branding and marketing led to a surge in customer trust and long-term loyalty.

Key Elements of Chipotle's Rebrand:
Food Transparency and Ingredient Integrity
Chipotle shifted its focus to full transparency about where its food comes from, promoting the use of **fresh, locally sourced, and ethically raised ingredients**. This focus on transparency became a core element of the brand, helping to reestablish trust with consumers who had lost confidence in the company.

Impact: By 2020, 85% of Chipotle's ingredients were sourced sustainably, and all its dairy and meats came from ethically raised animals. This commitment to sustainability became a key differentiator in the crowded fast-casual space.

Commitment to Sustainability
Chipotle embedded sustainability into its brand ethos, focusing on environmental responsibility as a core part of its message. From compostable bowls to waste reduction programs, the brand's identity became synonymous with being **eco-conscious**.

Impact: Chipotle's environmental initiatives resonated strongly with consumers. In 2021, the brand launched its Real Foodprint tool, which lets customers see the environmental impact of their meal choices. This tool demonstrated Chipotle's long-term commitment to sustainability, increasing its credibility with eco-conscious consumers.

Branding Beyond Products: Building a Purpose-Driven Identity

Chipotle's branding wasn't just about what they sold; it was about why they existed. The company's **"food with integrity"** mission gave it a clear purpose that resonated with customers who cared about what they were eating and how it was sourced.

Impact: By creating a purpose-driven brand, Chipotle attracted a new wave of loyal customers. By 2022, **digital sales increased to 45.6%** of total sales, with many customers attracted to Chipotle's messaging around transparency and sustainability. This rise in digital sales was a direct reflection of the brand's strengthened identity.

Branding Is Essential

Chipotle's rebranding wasn't just theoretical; it was backed by marketing campaigns that tied directly to its brand ethos, proving that branding is not just measurable but critical for long-term growth.

1. "For Real" Campaign (2018-2020)

One of the cornerstone marketing campaigns of Chipotle's rebrand was the **"For Real"** campaign, which emphasized the company's commitment to using **33 real ingredients** that customers could recognize and trust. The campaign highlighted the simplicity of Chipotle's food and its focus on using only ingredients with a **transparent supply chain**.

Impact: The campaign successfully rebuilt consumer trust, leading to a **9% increase in same-store sales** by 2020, which marked one of the strongest sales rebounds in the company's history. Chipotle's transparent messaging around real ingredients not only increased customer trust but also allowed the brand to differentiate itself from fast-food competitors.

2. "Behind the Foil" Campaign (2020)

To further its brand messaging, Chipotle launched the **"Behind the Foil"** campaign in 2020, which took customers behind the scenes of its kitchen. The campaign focused on showing **authentic, unfiltered moments** of how Chipotle sources and prepares its food, reinforcing the brand's commitment to transparency and quality.

Impact: The "Behind the Foil" campaign led to **12.3% year-over-year revenue growth** in 2021, showcasing how branding built around transparency and realness can create measurable results. The campaign also contributed to Chipotle's impressive growth in **digital sales**, which doubled to $1 billion in 2020.

3. Sustainability Initiatives and Real Foodprint (2021)

In 2021, Chipotle launched its **Real Foodprint** initiative, a sustainability dashboard that showed customers the positive environmental impact of choosing Chipotle over other fast-food options. This innovation aligned with Chipotle's brand identity of **sustainability and integrity**, giving customers an interactive way to connect with the brand's mission.

Impact: The Real Foodprint initiative not only increased **brand awareness** but also helped Chipotle stand out as a leader in the sustainable food space. The branding campaign saw strong engagement across digital platforms, with customers sharing their foodprint scores on social media, further expanding Chipotle's brand reach.

How Branding Drove Chipotle's Growth

While Chipotle's marketing campaigns were effective, it was the **cohesive brand identity** that allowed these campaigns to resonate deeply with consumers. Branding and marketing were intertwined—marketing drove awareness, but branding built trust, loyalty, and repeat business.

Metrics Highlighting Chipotle's Branding Success:

Revenue Growth: From 2017 to 2022, Chipotle's revenues increased from **$4.5 billion to $7.5 billion**, demonstrating how its rebranding efforts led to significant business growth.

Customer Loyalty and Retention: Chipotle's **Chipotle Rewards** program, launched in 2019, reached **over 28 million members** by 2022. The program's success can be attributed to the brand's ability to create an emotional connection with customers who value its commitment to quality and sustainability.

Digital Sales Explosion: By focusing on its brand message and integrating it with digital experiences, Chipotle's **digital sales skyrocketed** from $483 million in 2019 to **$3.4 billion in 2021**.

Chipotle's rebranding after its 2015-2016 crisis showcases the essential role branding plays in business success. Marketing alone couldn't have achieved the long-term recovery and growth that Chipotle experienced. By aligning its brand around **"food with integrity"** and reinforcing that identity with strategic marketing campaigns, Chipotle not only rebuilt its reputation but also positioned itself as a leader in the fast-casual space.

The numbers don't lie—Chipotle's **commitment to branding** has led to measurable success, from increased revenue and customer retention to expanded digital sales. This case study highlights the reality that **branding is not just necessary**—it's critical for long-term growth, loyalty, and differentiation.

Breaking Through the Myths

Branding is one of the most powerful tools you have as a business owner, but to harness its full potential, you need to break free from these common myths. Remember, branding is more than just a logo; it's an ongoing process of building trust, creating emotional connections, and telling your story in a way that resonates with your audience.

It doesn't have to be expensive, and it certainly isn't just fluff—branding has a direct impact on your sales, customer loyalty, and business growth. As you move forward in this book, we'll dive deeper into the strategies and practical steps you can take to create a brand that stands out, grows with your business, and drives success.

CHAPTER WORKSHEET: THE 5 MYTHS OF BRANDING

Use this worksheet to reflect on the 5 common myths of branding.

MYTH 1: BRANDING IS JUST A LOGO

Reality: Branding goes far beyond a logo. It encompasses the emotions, values, and experiences that define your business in the minds of your audience.

Reflect: In what ways have you focused too much on the visual aspects of your brand (e.g. logo, colors, type) rather than the deeper meaning and emotional connections you need to be building with your audience over time?

Write your response:

___

Action Step:

Identify one way you can enhance your brand's emotional connection with your audience (e.g., through storytelling, aligning with their values, or improving customer experience).

Write your response:

___

MYTH 2: BRANDING IS EXPENSIVE

Reality: Building a strong brand doesn't require a large budget. Consistency, authenticity, and creativity can help you build a powerful brand, even on a small budget.

Reflect: Where have you felt that branding was out of reach due to financial constraints? What low-cost branding strategies have you used, or can you use in the future (e.g., storytelling, social media engagement)?

Write your response:

```



```

Action Step:

Identify one affordable strategy you can implement to strengthen your brand, such as creating more engaging content or improving customer interactions.

Write your response:

```



```

MYTH 3: BRANDING DOESN'T IMPACT SALES

Reality: A strong brand creates loyalty, differentiates you from competitors, and directly influences purchasing decisions.

Reflect: Have you been overlooking the connection between your brand and sales? Think about a time when your brand's reputation or emotional connection helped close a sale. How did branding play a role?

Write your response:

```



```

Action Step:
List one way you can strengthen the link between your brand and your sales efforts (e.g., incorporating your brand's story into your sales pitch, improving customer service to reflect brand values).

Write your response:

```



```

MYTH 4: BRANDING CANNOT BE MEASURED
Reality: Branding is measurable through metrics like brand awareness, customer loyalty, and engagement.

Reflect: How have you been measuring your brand's success so far? Are you using key branding metrics (e.g., social media engagement, customer retention rates, brand mentions)?

Write your response:

```


```

Choose one metric to start tracking (e.g., brand awareness, customer loyalty, engagement rates) and describe how you will measure it.

Write your response:

```


```

MYTH 5: BRANDING ISN'T NECESSARY BUT MARKETING IS

Reality: Branding and marketing work hand in hand. Branding defines the message; marketing communicates it. Without branding, your marketing lacks direction and meaning.

Reflect: Have you been focused more on marketing than on building a consistent brand? How can you better align your marketing tactics with your brand values?

Write your response:

```


```

Action Step:
Identify one way to improve the alignment between your branding and marketing (e.g., refining your messaging, ensuring your visuals reflect your brand's core values).

Write your response:

```
```

FINAL REFLECTION
After completing this worksheet, consider: How has your understanding of branding evolved? What myths do you need to overcome in your own business? Reflect and summarize your thoughts:

```
```

By working through this recap, you've taken important steps to ensure that your brand reflects your core values, connect

CHAPTER 3:
DEFINING YOUR BRAND'S IDENTITY—THE POWER OF YOUR ORIGIN STORY

"Every business wants their consumers to feel emotionally invested, to see their product or service as more than a transaction but as something that enhances their lives, shapes their identity, and speaks to their values."

I believe that every strong brand identity begins with a compelling **origin story**. Your brand identity isn't just about visuals or messaging; it's about the deep-rooted narrative that informs how you present yourself to the world. It's the story of how your brand came to be, the challenges you overcame, and the mission that drives you. Your **origin story** becomes the foundation upon which every element of your brand identity is built. It's the source of authenticity, the reason your audience connects with you, and the driving force behind why they choose your brand over others.

When you create a brand people believe in, it's not just because of what you sell—it's because of the story behind it. Your **brand identity** is the outward expression of that story, and this is what shapes the way your customers feel about your business. When done right, it's what transforms your brand from just another company into something that feels personal, relatable, and unforgettable.

Why Your Origin Story is Central to Brand Identity
Your **origin story** is the emotional heartbeat of your brand. It's not just where you came from—it's the reason your business exists and the journey that got you here. For your audience, the origin story answers the question: *Why should I care?*

When people understand where your brand comes from and what drives it, they're more likely to form a meaningful connection. Your origin story makes your brand human, relatable, and authentic. It gives your customers something to believe in beyond just the products or services you offer.

Think of **Apple**, whose origin story started in Steve Jobs' garage. That story isn't just about where Apple physically began; it's about a mindset of innovation, risk-taking, and challenging the status quo. The garage became a symbol of creativity and revolution, and Apple's brand identity has been built around that narrative ever since. For your brand, the origin story is the first chapter in a much larger book—the one that customers will read as they engage with you.

Business vs. Personal Brand Identity:
The Intersection of Story and Strategy

For entrepreneurs, brand identity exists on two levels: the business brand and the personal brand. Each serves a different purpose, but both are vital to how your audience connects with you.

Every business has a brand identity, whether it's intentional or not. But as an entrepreneur, you also have a personal brand identity—your individual presence, reputation, and the values you represent. Both business and personal brand identities are important, but they serve different purposes.

- √ **Business Brand Identity**: This is how your company presents itself to the world. It includes your company's mission, values, and visual assets like your logo, website design, and messaging. A business brand identity is designed to connect with your target audience and create a consistent, recognizable presence.

- √ **Personal Brand Identity**: Your personal brand is how *you*, as an entrepreneur or leader, are perceived by others. It includes your personality, expertise, and how you communicate your values to your audience. In some cases, especially for entrepreneurs, the personal brand and the business brand are closely intertwined. Think of individuals like Elon Musk or Oprah Winfrey, where the person is often inseparable from the business.

Business Brand Identity: Your business brand identity is how your company presents itself to the world. It includes your mission, vision, values, and the visual and emotional elements that communicate your brand's story. Your origin story plays a crucial role here because it gives your business identity depth and meaning.

For example, if your business started because you saw a gap in the market that no one was addressing, your brand identity should emphasize innovation, problem-solving, and customer-focused solutions. The way you express this through your visuals, messaging, and customer interactions all stem from that initial narrative.

Personal Brand Identity: For entrepreneurs and small business owners, your personal brand is often intertwined with your business brand. People don't just buy into your products—they buy into *you*. Your personal journey, values, and expertise all contribute to your brand's identity.

Think about individuals like **Oprah Winfrey** or **Elon Musk**—their personal brands are inseparable from the businesses they lead. Your origin story as an entrepreneur—the risks you took, the challenges you faced, and the passion that drives you—is just as important as your business story. Customers often buy into your vision and character as much as they buy into your product.

When your personal and business brand identities align, they create a powerful connection with your audience.

Crafting a Strong Brand Identity Through the Creation and Use of Your Origin Story

A strong brand identity is built on more than just visuals and marketing strategies—it's about telling a story that resonates with your audience. Your origin story is the foundation, but your mission, vision, values, and unique selling proposition (USP) are the pillars that hold it up. These elements should all connect back to the story of how and why your brand came to life.

Before you start crafting the different elements of your brand identity, ask yourself these essential questions:

1. **Who is my target audience?**
   Who are you trying to reach? What values do they hold, and how do you want your story to resonate with them? Understanding your audience is the first step to ensuring your brand identity aligns with their needs and desires.

2. **What problem does my business solve?**
   Your brand identity should reflect how you solve a specific problem for your customers. Your origin story should highlight how you identified this problem and why your solution is unique. Customers want to know that you understand

their challenges and can help them overcome them.

3. **What makes my business different?**
Differentiation is key. What sets your brand apart from others? Your origin story is a great place to showcase the unique experiences and insights that led you to create something different from the competition.

4. **What emotions do I want my brand to evoke?**
Branding is about creating an emotional connection with your audience. Your origin story should evoke emotions like trust, excitement, or inspiration. Think about how you want people to feel when they engage with your brand.

5. **What are my core values?**
Your core values guide your brand's decisions and behaviors. They should be reflected in your origin story and be consistent throughout your brand's identity. Customers are more likely to trust and stay loyal to brands whose values align with their own.

BRANDING
THE GOLDEN CIRCLE

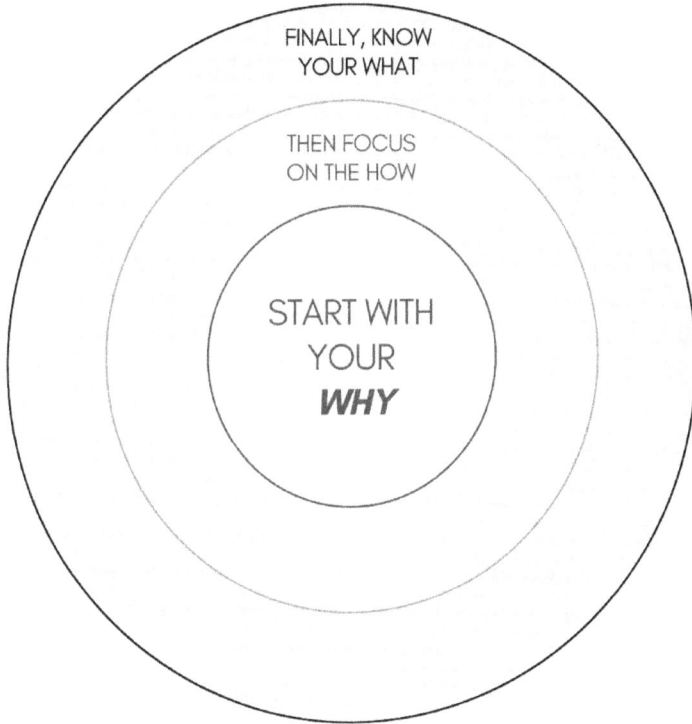

FINALLY, KNOW
YOUR WHAT

THEN FOCUS
ON THE HOW

START WITH
YOUR
WHY

thisisbrandingbook.com

**Example: Defining Brand Identity with the Origin
Story – Meet EcoClean**

To see how this works in practice, let's look
at **EcoClean,** a cleaning product company that provides
eco-friendly cleaning products. EcoClean's founder,
Sarah, started the business after discovering that the
products she was using to clean her home were harmful
to her family's health and the environment. She decided

to create an alternative—one that was safe, effective, and sustainable.

Mission: The Immediate Why
EcoClean's mission statement is grounded in Sarah's personal journey and the problem she set out to solve. The mission is to provide safe, eco-friendly cleaning products that protect both families and the environment.

Mission: "EcoClean provides environmentally friendly cleaning solutions that protect your home and the planet, ensuring a healthy and toxin-free environment for your family."

Vision: The Long-Term Aspiration
The vision statement looks beyond the immediate problem and expresses the brand's long-term goal. Sarah's vision is to lead a global movement toward sustainable living, one household at a time.
Vision: "To lead the global movement towards sustainable living, one clean home at a time."

Values: The Guiding Principles
EcoClean's values reflect Sarah's commitment to sustainability, health, and integrity—principles that were key motivators in her personal journey. These values guide everything the company does, from product development to customer service.

Values:
- **Sustainability**: We prioritize eco-friendly practices in every aspect of our business.

- **Health**: We believe in promoting healthier living by eliminating toxins from homes.
- **Integrity**: We are committed to transparency and honesty in all our products and business practices.

Crafting Your Unique Selling Proposition (USP)

Your **unique selling proposition (USP)** should flow naturally from your origin story. It's what makes your brand stand out in a crowded market, and it tells your audience why they should choose you over anyone else. Your USP should highlight the unique benefit your brand offers, and why that benefit is meaningful in the context of your story.

For EcoClean, Sarah's journey of discovering harmful toxins in everyday cleaning products informs the company's USP. EcoClean isn't just another cleaning product; it's a solution built on personal experience, driven by a desire to protect families and the environment.

USP: "EcoClean is the only cleaning brand that combines 100% plant-based ingredients with cutting-edge technology to deliver powerful, non-toxic cleaning solutions that are safe for both your family and the environment." This USP ties directly back to Sarah's story, highlighting EcoClean's commitment to safety, innovation, and sustainability. It's not just about selling a product—it's about selling a solution customers can trust.

Creating a Clear Brand Statement

Finally, your brand statement ties everything together—your mission, vision, values, and USP—into one cohesive message that communicates what your brand stands for. Your brand statement should be simple, memorable, and rooted in your origin story. It's the one sentence that captures the essence of your brand and can be used across all platforms.

Brand Statement (EcoClean):

EcoClean empowers families to live healthier lives with eco-friendly, plant-based cleaning solutions that protect the home and the planet—because sustainability and health shouldn't be compromised.

This brand statement captures EcoClean's mission to provide eco-friendly solutions, its commitment to health and sustainability, and its unique selling proposition. It's a clear, concise message that ties back to the origin story of why Sarah started.

Your brand identity is the expression of your origin story, woven into every facet of your business. By defining your mission, vision, values, and USP, you're building a brand that's authentic, memorable, and capable of creating deep connections with your audience. This is where branding starts—with a story, your story. As you move forward, remember that everything you build should reflect that foundational narrative, ensuring that your brand feels real, relatable, and unforgettable.

Your brand identity is the embodiment of your story.

Rooted in your mission, vision, and values.

It should be authentic, relatable, and unforgettable.

UNEARTHING YOUR BRAND'S MISSION: A mission statement is a concise expression of your business's core purpose and focus, serving as the foundation upon which your brand is built. It articulates why your business exists, who it serves, and what it strives to accomplish.

WHY IT MATTERS:
√ **Direction and Focus:** It keeps your business focused on its core purpose, ensuring that all efforts and initiatives are aligned with what you stand for.
√ **Employee Alignment and Motivation:** It provides your team with a clear understanding of the business's goals and their role in achieving them, fostering a sense of belonging and purpose.
√ **Customer Connection:** It helps customers understand what your business is about and why they should care, building a deeper emotional connection with your brand.

THE EXERCISE: Reflect on the fundamental elements that define your business. What is the change you seek to make in your customers' lives, and how do you achieve this? Using the guidance above, write a mission statement that succinctly captures the essence of your business.

REFLECTION: After crafting your mission statement, take a moment to consider its implications for your business operations, marketing strategies, and customer engagement. Does your current business model align with this mission? How can you better integrate your mission into every aspect of your brand experience?

ENVISIONING THE FUTURE: A vision statement is a forward-looking declaration that outlines what your business aspires to be in the future. It serves as a roadmap for where you want your brand to go, reflecting your ambitions and defining the long-term objectives of your business. Unlike a mission statement, which focuses on the present and describes the purpose of your business, a vision statement is about setting a direction for the future growth and impact of your brand.

WHY IT MATTERS:
√ **Inspiration and Motivation:** It inspires you, your team, and your customers by painting a picture of the impact your business seeks to make.
√ **Strategic Alignment:** It ensures every decision and strategy aligns with where you want your brand to be in the future, keeping your business on track.
√ **Culture and Identity:** It helps in shaping the culture of your organization, fostering a strong brand identity.

THE EXCERCISE: Take some time to reflect on the impact you want your brand to have in the future. Consider the aspirations you have for your business and how you want it to be perceived. With those thoughts in mind, craft a vision statement.

```
[blank box]
```

REFLECTION: Once you've crafted your vision statement, reflect on how it aligns with your current brand strategies and actions. Does your current path lead you toward this vision? What changes or innovations might be necessary to make this vision a reality?

```
[blank box]
```

YOUR BRAND'S PURPOSE

Defining your brand's purpose goes beyond identifying what your business does or sells; it's about understanding the deeper reason your brand exists in the first place. Your brand's purpose is the bridge between your mission (the present focus) and your vision (the future aspiration). It embodies the impact you wish to have on your customers and the wider world and incorporates your origin story.

WHY IT MATTERS:

1. **Emotional Connection:** A clear, purpose-driven brand resonates more deeply with customers,

employees, and stakeholders by aligning with their values and aspirations.

2. **Differentiation:** In a saturated market, your brand's purpose can set you apart, not just by what you do but by why you do it.

3. **Longevity and Resilience:** Brands with a strong sense of purpose are better equipped to navigate market changes and challenges because they're anchored in something deeper than just products or services.

THE EXERCISE: Combine insights from your mission and vision exercises with the broader impact and emotional drivers you've identified. Craft a statement that defines why your brand exists beyond making a profit.

REFLECTION: With your brand's purpose articulated, consider whether there are areas where your purpose could be more deeply integrated? How can ensuring alignment with your purpose across all touchpoints enhance your brand's strength and coherence?

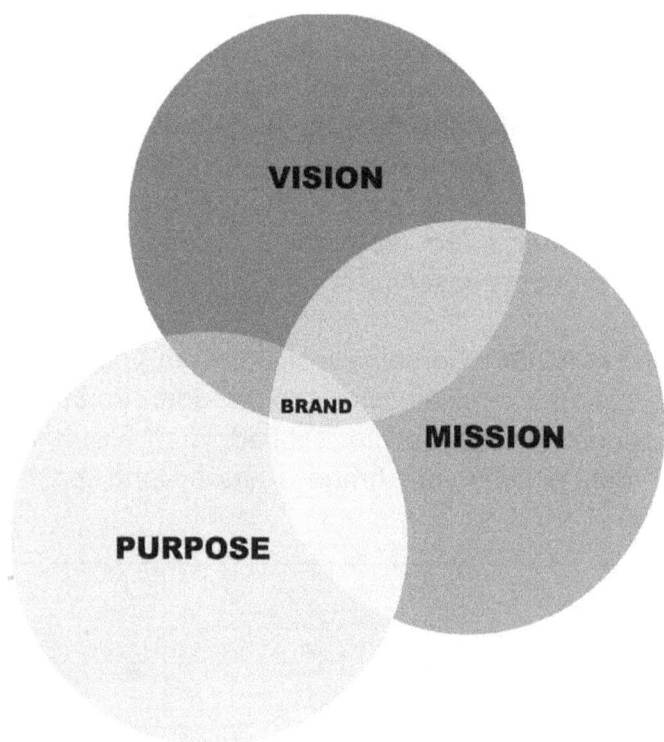

FIG. 1: UNDERSTANDING HOW THEY ALL INTERSECT

CHAPTER 4: LEVERAGING BRAND PSYCHOLOGY FOR GROWTH – THE POWER OF PURPOSE

"But how do brands inspire such loyalty? What makes people feel connected to Starbucks in a way they don't feel toward another coffee chain with similar offerings? It's not just about marketing, great locations, or excellent customer service—though those help. It's about the story that the brand tells and the emotional connection it builds over time"

Brand psychology is the art of understanding how your audience thinks, feels, and responds to your brand. But to truly leverage that psychology for growth, you must start by defining and conveying your purpose—the core reason your brand exists. A brand's purpose goes beyond selling a product or service; it's about standing for something larger that resonates with your audience on a personal and emotional level. When your audience believes in your purpose, they don't just buy your products—they buy into your brand's values, identity, and story.

In this chapter, we'll explore how mastering brand psychology through purpose-driven branding can create meaningful connections that inspire loyalty, build long-term relationships, and foster growth. Your purpose is the foundation of everything your brand stands for, and when it's conveyed authentically and clearly, it becomes the driving force behind customer engagement, loyalty, and advocacy.

The Modes of Emotional Branding

Aristotle's concept of emotional persuasion, often referred to as "rhetorical appeals," consists of three key modes: **ethos**, **pathos**, and **logos**. These principles have been adapted into modern emotional branding to create deeper connections with audiences.

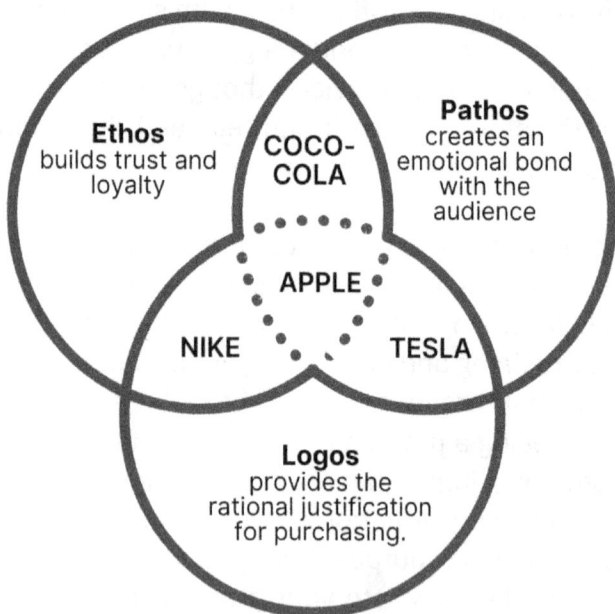

Ethos
builds trust and loyalty

COCO-COLA

Pathos
creates an emotional bond with the audience

APPLE

NIKE · · TESLA

Logos
provides the rational justification for purchasing.

thisisbrandingbook.com

The Importance of Purpose in Brand Psychology
At the heart of brand psychology is understanding that people don't just buy products; they buy what those products represent. This is where purpose comes into play. Purpose-driven brands stand for something beyond profit—they reflect values, solve meaningful problems, and provide a sense of belonging or identity for their customers. When you clearly convey your brand's purpose, you tap into a powerful emotional connection that encourages customers to align with your brand because they believe in the same values.

Consider **Starbucks**: It's not just a coffee chain; it's a brand built on the purpose of fostering connection and community. The company's mission, "to inspire and nurture the human spirit—one person, one cup, and one neighborhood at a time," reflects more than just serving coffee. It's about creating spaces where people feel welcome and connected. This purpose resonates deeply with their customers, fostering loyalty and trust.

Author's Insight
A brand's purpose is its soul. It's what gives your brand meaning beyond the transaction, and it's what turns customers into lifelong supporters. When you define and communicate your purpose clearly, you give people a reason to believe in your brand.

Emotional Branding: Connecting Through Purpose
Emotional branding is about tapping into your audience's feelings by creating experiences and messages that evoke specific emotions. A clear and authentic purpose is essential for effective emotional branding because it gives customers a reason to care.

When your brand stands for something that aligns with their values, your customers will feel emotionally connected, which drives loyalty and engagement.

For example, a purpose-driven brand like **TOMS Shoes** doesn't just sell footwear—it stands for giving back. Their "One for One" campaign, which donates a pair of shoes to a child in need for every pair purchased, is rooted in the brand's purpose of making the world a better place. This simple but powerful purpose creates an emotional bond with customers, who feel like they're part of something bigger when they make a purchase.

How to Use Emotional Branding to Convey Purpose

√ **Understand Your Audience's Values**: To create emotional connections, first understand what your audience cares about. What values do they hold? What problems do they face? Use surveys, focus groups, and social listening to get insights into their emotional needs.

√ **Tell Your Brand's Story**: Your brand's origin story is a powerful tool for emotional branding. Share how your purpose came to be, the challenges you faced, and the values that drive you. Authentic storytelling makes your brand relatable and human.

√ **Align Your Brand with a Bigger Cause**: Brands that stand for something bigger than themselves naturally create stronger emotional connections. Whether your purpose is tied to sustainability, social justice, or innovation, make sure it's a key part of your messaging and actions.

√ **Use Emotionally Driven Language**: The words you choose in your messaging should evoke the emotions you want to associate with your brand. If your purpose is about empowerment, use inspiring and motivating language. If it's about comfort or safety, choose warm, reassuring words.

This is Branding Example: Dove

Dove's **Real Beauty** campaign is one of the most successful examples of emotional branding. The campaign doesn't just sell soap—it sells self-confidence and body positivity. Dove's purpose, rooted in challenging beauty stereotypes and promoting self-acceptance, taps into the emotions of their audience, making customers feel empowered and supported in a deep underlying problem that they themselves are sometimes too scared to even acknowledge. By aligning with this purpose, Dove created an emotional connection with its audience that goes far beyond its products.

Author's Insight

Emotional branding isn't about manipulating feelings; it's about genuinely understanding what your audience cares about and reflecting that in your brand's purpose. When your purpose aligns with your customers' values, the emotional connection is real—and lasting.

The Role of Visuals in Conveying Purpose

Visual branding is a critical part of brand psychology because it communicates your purpose without words. Your logo, color palette, typography, and design choices should all reflect the essence of your brand's purpose. Humans process visuals much faster than text, and those visuals trigger subconscious emotional responses. By choosing the right visual elements, you can reinforce your purpose and connect with your audience on an emotional level from the moment they see your brand.

How to Use Visual Branding to Reflect Purpose
1. **Choose Colors that Represent Your Purpose**: Colors have a powerful impact on emotions. Choose colors that align with the message your brand's purpose is trying to convey. For example:
   - √ **Green** is often associated with health, nature, and sustainability—perfect for a purpose-driven brand focused on eco-friendliness, like **EcoClean**.
   - √ **Red** represents passion and excitement and is commonly used by brands that want to evoke bold emotions, such as **Coca-Cola**.
   - √ **Blue** conveys trust, professionalism, and calmness, making it ideal for brands focused on reliability and safety, like **PayPal** or healthcare brands.
2. **Use Shapes and Typography to Convey Your Brand Personality**:
   Rounded shapes and soft lines tend to feel more friendly and approachable, while sharp angles and clean lines communicate strength and precision. Similarly, typography choices can influence how your brand is perceived. Serif fonts convey tradition and trust, while sans-serif fonts feel modern and innovative.
3. **Be Consistent Across All Visual Touchpoints**:
   Consistency is crucial for building a strong visual identity that reflects your purpose. Whether your audience encounters your brand on social media, your website, or in physical stores, the

visual experience should be cohesive and immediately recognizable.

This is Branding Example: EcoClean
Remember EcoClean, our cleaning products company mentioned in Chapter 3 offering eco-friendly cleaning options? It uses **green** as its primary color to evoke feelings of sustainability and health. Its logo features a simple leaf design, reinforcing the brand's commitment to nature and eco-conscious living. Across all touchpoints, from packaging to the website, the consistent use of nature-inspired imagery, calming fonts, and clean layouts conveys the brand's purpose of protecting both people and the planet.

Author's Insight

Your brand's visuals are like a first impression—they tell your audience what your brand stands for before you even say a word. Make sure your colors, logos, and designs reflect your purpose clearly and consistently. It's the first step in building trust.

Positioning Your Brand for Long-Term Loyalty through Purpose
Brand positioning is about carving out a unique space in the market where your brand can thrive, and your **purpose** is at the heart of that positioning. When customers know what you stand for, and when your values align with theirs, they are more likely to stay loyal to your brand for the long haul.

How to Position Your Brand Around Your Purpose
1. **Know Your Audience and Their Values**: Positioning begins with understanding your

audience. What do they care about, and how does your brand's purpose connect with their values? For example, if your audience is environmentally conscious, position your brand as the go-to for sustainable products that don't compromise on quality, like **EcoClean**.

2. **Make Your Purpose Clear in Every Touchpoint**: Your purpose should be evident in everything you do, from your marketing messages to your customer service approach. When customers interact with your brand, they should immediately understand what you stand for and why they should choose you.

3. **Deliver on Your Promise Consistently**: Long-term loyalty is built on trust, and trust comes from delivering on your brand's purpose consistently. Make sure your products, services, and customer experiences align with your brand's values and purpose every time. When customers know they can rely on you to uphold your brand's promises, they are more likely to stay loyal.

4. **Engage Your Community Around a Shared Purpose**:
Brands that build communities around their purpose often enjoy stronger loyalty. Use your brand's purpose to create a sense of belonging and connection among your audience. Engage with them on social media, offer exclusive content or experiences for loyal customers, and encourage user-generated content that reinforces your purpose.

This is Branding Example: Nike

Nike's brand positioning is centered around its purpose of **empowerment through sports**. The famous "Just Do It" slogan isn't just about physical activity—it's about overcoming challenges, pushing limits, and striving for greatness. Nike consistently delivers this message through its products, campaigns, and community engagement. By positioning itself as a brand that helps people reach their full potential, Nike has created a community of loyal customers who believe in the brand's purpose and live by its message.

Author's Insight

Loyalty isn't just about offering a great product—it's about giving your audience a reason to believe in you. When your purpose is clear and resonates with your audience, they'll choose you not because you're the cheapest or closest option, but because they believe in what you stand for.

Mastering Brand Psychology Through Purpose: Driving Growth and Loyalty

To truly master **brand psychology**, your brand's purpose must be more than just a statement—it must be the emotional core that drives all your actions, decisions, and messaging. Purpose is the invisible thread that connects every aspect of your brand with your audience on a deeper, more meaningful level. When customers align with your purpose, they don't just buy your products—they become emotionally invested in your brand, creating the foundation for long-term loyalty and sustained growth.

In this section, we'll dive deeper into how mastering brand psychology through purpose can help you build emotional connections, foster trust, and create a community of advocates who are passionate about your brand. The goal is not just to sell but to build a brand that your customers love and want to support.

1. Be Authentic and Transparent

Authenticity is the cornerstone of any purpose-driven brand. Today's consumers are savvier than ever, and they can quickly spot when a brand is being inauthentic or merely jumping on the latest trend to appear relevant. For your purpose to resonate, it must be genuine, deeply rooted in your brand's values, and consistently reflected in everything you do.

Customers want to support brands that are honest and transparent about what they stand for. They expect authenticity, whether you're talking about your commitment to sustainability, inclusivity, or innovation. It's not enough to simply declare a purpose; you must live it, and every interaction with your brand should reinforce that commitment.

So, Really How Do You Show Authenticity?
√ **Walk the Walk:** Don't just talk about your brand's purpose—embed it in your company culture and operations. For example, if your purpose is sustainability, this should be reflected in your sourcing, manufacturing processes, packaging, and even how you treat your employees. Authenticity means backing up your words with meaningful action.

- √ **Share Your Story:** Be transparent about your journey. Customers appreciate honesty, even about your brand's struggles and challenges. Sharing the hurdles you've overcome to stay true to your purpose humanizes your brand and makes it relatable. The more open and authentic you are, the stronger the connection with your audience.
- √ **Maintain Consistency:** Your purpose should be reflected consistently across all touchpoints— whether it's on your website, in your marketing campaigns, or during customer service interactions. Authenticity can't be seasonal or situational; it must be ever-present in your brand's DNA.

This is Branding Example: Patagonia

Patagonia, the outdoor clothing brand, has built its entire identity around environmental sustainability. Their purpose is clear: to save the planet through responsible business practices. Patagonia doesn't just promote this message; they live it. From pledging 1% of sales to environmental causes to encouraging customers to repair, rather than replace, their gear, Patagonia's authenticity shines through in every aspect of their business. This transparency has earned them fierce loyalty and respect from consumers who value the environment as much as they do.

2. Create Emotional Triggers Around Your Purpose

At the heart of brand psychology is the ability to create emotional triggers that make customers feel something when they think of your brand. Purpose-driven brands are especially powerful in evoking emotions because they tap into values and beliefs that are important to their customers. Whether it's a sense of belonging, hope, empowerment, or responsibility, emotions are the glue that binds customers to your brand.

How to Create Emotional Triggers:

√ **Use Storytelling:** One of the most effective ways to tap into emotion is through storytelling. Share the origin of your purpose, the stories of people your brand has helped, or how your customers are making a difference by supporting your brand. Stories humanize your purpose and allow your audience to emotionally connect with it.

√ **Evoke Specific Emotions:** Identify the key emotions that align with your purpose and make them central to your messaging. For example, if your brand's purpose revolves around empowerment, use inspirational language, visuals, and stories that make your customers feel like they can achieve greatness by choosing your brand. If your purpose is related to comfort or safety, craft messages that evoke feelings of reassurance and trust.

√ **Create Purposeful Experiences:** Beyond words and visuals, your brand's actions can trigger emotional responses. This could be through charitable donations, community-building initiatives, or even product packaging that tells a story. Consider how every interaction a customer has with your brand can trigger positive emotions that align with your purpose.

This is Branding Example: Nike
Nike's purpose is centered on **empowerment through sport,** and they consistently create emotional triggers that inspire their customers to push their limits. The "Just Do It" campaign is a perfect example—Nike doesn't just sell shoes; they sell a message of perseverance and personal achievement. Through powerful storytelling, like featuring athletes who've overcome adversity, Nike taps into emotions of determination, grit, and empowerment. This connection goes far beyond the product, creating an emotional bond that keeps customers coming back.

3. Align Every Aspect of Your Brand with Your Purpose
To fully master brand psychology through purpose, your brand must be in complete alignment with that purpose at every touchpoint. Whether a customer is interacting with your website, your social media channels, or your product packaging, they should immediately understand what your brand stands for. When everything aligns with your purpose, it creates a seamless, cohesive brand experience that deepens trust and strengthens your relationship with customers.

How to Ensure Alignment:
- √ **Internal Culture and External Messaging:** Your brand's purpose shouldn't just be an external marketing tool—it should be a core part of your company's internal culture. Ensure that your employees, partners, and even suppliers understand and support your purpose. This internal alignment will reflect in the authenticity of your external messaging.

- √ **Product Development and Design:** Every product or service you create should reflect your purpose. For example, if your brand stands for innovation, each new product should push boundaries and showcase creativity. If your purpose is environmental sustainability, your product design, packaging, and production methods should align with eco-friendly practices.
- √ **Customer Interactions:** Whether online or in person, how your team interacts with customers should reinforce your brand's purpose. If your purpose is centered on customer empowerment, your customer service should go above and beyond to make customers feel valued and heard.

This is Branding Example: Warby Parker

Warby Parker's purpose is to provide high-quality eyewear at an affordable price, while also making a positive social impact. Their business model aligns perfectly with this purpose: for every pair of glasses sold, they donate a pair to someone in need. The entire customer experience, from their website to their in-store service, reflects a focus on quality, accessibility, and giving back. By aligning every aspect of their brand with their purpose, Warby Parker has built a loyal customer base that believes in both their products and their mission.

4. Foster a Community Around Your Purpose

A brand with a clear, compelling purpose has the unique ability to build a community around shared value. Communities provide a sense of belonging, and when customers feel that they are part of something larger than themselves, they become more than just buyers— they become advocates for your brand. The most successful brands not only foster these communities but actively engage with them, turning their purpose into a movement that customers want to be a part of.

How to Build a Purpose-Driven Community:
- √ **Create Opportunities for Engagement:** Build platforms where your customers can engage with your brand and with each other. This could be through social media groups, forums, or in-person events. Encourage discussions, user-generated content, and feedback that make your customers feel like valued members of your brand's community.
- √ **Give Your Audience a Voice:** Empower your customers to contribute to your brand's purpose. Whether it's through online reviews, testimonials, or even product design input, giving your audience a voice strengthens their emotional connection to your brand.
- √ **Reward Loyalty:** Show appreciation to your most loyal customers by offering exclusive rewards, early access to products, or special discounts. When people feel recognized for their support, they're more likely to remain loyal and advocate for your brand.

This is Branding Example: Lululemon
Lululemon, the activewear brand, has built a thriving community around its purpose of promoting health, wellness, and mindfulness. They host in-store yoga classes, sponsor community events, and engage

customers through their **"SweatLife"** movement, which promotes an active, balanced lifestyle. By fostering this community, Lululemon has created more than just a brand; they've created a lifestyle that their customers are eager to be a part of.

Driving Growth and Loyalty Through Purpose
When you master brand psychology by fully embracing and communicating your purpose, you unlock the key to driving sustained growth and building long-term loyalty. Customers don't just buy from purpose-driven brands— they believe in them. They become advocates, they tell their friends and family, and they stay loyal even when competitors come knocking.

Here's how mastering purpose can fuel your brand's growth:

√ **Increased Customer Loyalty:** Purpose-driven brands see higher levels of loyalty because customers feel emotionally connected. When customers believe in your purpose, they're more likely to stick with your brand, even when they have other options.

√ **Word-of-Mouth Marketing:** Customers who believe in your brand's purpose are more likely to recommend it to others. This advocacy can lead to organic growth through word-of-mouth referrals and social media sharing.

√ **Differentiation in a Crowded Market:** A well-defined purpose helps you stand out in a saturated market. When competitors focus solely on product features, your brand's purpose can be the differentiator that draws customers to you instead.

√ **Attracting Purpose-Driven Talent:** Brands with a clear purpose don't just attract loyal customers—they attract passionate employees. People want to work for companies that align with their values, and by living your purpose, you'll attract talent that is equally invested in your mission.

By mastering brand psychology through purpose, you create a brand that resonates with customers on an emotional level, fosters loyalty, and drives long-term growth. Purpose isn't just a buzzword—it's the foundation for building a brand that stands the test of time.

Author's Insight

Growth doesn't come from selling more—it comes from creating deeper connections. Your purpose is what turns customers into advocates, employees into ambassadors, and your brand into a movement. When you leverage your purpose authentically and consistently, you're not just building a brand—you're building something people believe in, and that's the true key to long-term success.

THE POWER OF PURPOSE WORKSHEET
UNDERSTANIDNG YOUR AUDIENCE'S NEEDS

Understanding and defining your target audience's needs, wants and core psychology is essential for creating a brand that resonates and communicates effectively. This worksheet will guide you through the process of uncovering what motivates them, and ensuring your brand aligns seamlessly with their needs.

THINK

Capture everything your ideal customer believes about your product or service and their problem area. Consider questions they might have, assumptions they're making, and their overall mindset.

FEEL

This section is about the emotions your ideal customer experiences during their interaction with your brand. Are they frustrated, hopeful, excited, or skeptical?

SEE

Now focus on what your customer sees in their environment that could influence their perception of your brand.

DO

Finally, the 'Do' quadrant captures the actions your target audience takes because of their thoughts, feelings, and what they see. This can include reaching out to your brand, making a purchase, seeking reviews, or even walking away.

CHAPTER 5: LEVERAGING SYMBOLS TO ENSURE BRAND CONSISTENCY

"Brands like Apple, Tesla, and Nike have mastered the idea of brand consistency. People don't just buy their products—they buy into their stories, their visions, and their ideals. It's not just about having the best product on the market; it's about creating a sense of belonging. Apple represents innovation and creativity; Tesla symbolizes a commitment to a sustainable future; Nike stands for perseverance and achievement. These brands tap into something deeper than the physical product. They tap into beliefs."

When building a brand, the symbols you choose—your logo, color palette, typography, and imagery—are more than just visual elements. They are representations of your brand's identity, values, and purpose. These symbols must not only convey the right message, but they must do so consistently across all platforms and touchpoints to build a cohesive brand experience. Brand consistency through the use of symbols ensures that whether a customer encounters your brand on social media, your website, or in-store, they have the same emotional and psychological response.

This chapter will delve into how you can use the power of symbols to maintain brand consistency across multiple channels. We'll explore why consistency is crucial for building trust and recognition, how to create a brand style guide to maintain it, and the automation tools you can leverage to ensure your symbols stay aligned everywhere your brand appears.

Consistency in Symbols Is Essential for Building Trust

Symbols, like your logo, colors, and typography, are the **visual shorthand** for your brand. They communicate your identity instantly and convey the emotions you want your audience to feel. Consistency in these symbols across every platform builds **trust** and helps create a cohesive brand experience. When customers see your brand represented the same way, every time, they begin to feel like they *know* your brand. This predictability fosters familiarity and trust, which are essential for creating long-term loyalty.

Why Is Consistency in Symbols Necessary?

People trust brands they recognize. When your visual identity is inconsistent—whether through different colors, fonts, or messaging—customers may feel confused or uncertain about your brand's professionalism. Inconsistent branding can make your business appear disjointed or unreliable. Conversely, when your brand shows up the same way across all channels, it strengthens brand recognition and builds trust, ensuring that customers feel confident in choosing you again and again.

The Benefits of Consistency in Symbols

Symbols are the cornerstone of your brand's visual identity, and consistency in how they are applied across all platforms delivers powerful benefits that drive brand recognition, trust, and loyalty. The symbols you use—your logo, colors, typography, and imagery—are the first impression people have of your brand. When they are applied consistently, they become instantly recognizable, making your brand memorable and reliable. Let's dive deeper into the key benefits of maintaining consistency in your brand's symbols:

1. Builds Trust

When your brand's symbols are used consistently, they create a sense of predictability. People feel more comfortable and confident when they know what to expect. Trust is built when customers see the same logo, colors, and tone of voice across every platform. Whether they're browsing your website, following your Instagram, or receiving an email from your brand, a cohesive identity reassures them that they're interacting with the same entity. For example, imagine visiting a website where the logo looks different from what you've seen on social media or an email where the colors don't match the brand's previous campaigns. These inconsistencies can make the brand seem unreliable or disorganized. On the other hand, when your branding is consistent, it reinforces your brand's credibility and professionalism, making customers feel confident in their choice to engage with you.

Why It Matters:
Consistency helps people feel secure in their purchasing decisions. If your branding is fragmented or inconsistent, it can lead to confusion, making customers question your reliability. Consistency in symbols is a silent agreement that says, "You can trust us."

2. Strengthens Brand Recognition
One of the most significant benefits of consistency in symbols is its impact on brand recognition. Over time, as people repeatedly encounter your brand's consistent visual identity, it becomes familiar to them. This familiarity is crucial for building a strong brand because the more people recognize your brand, the more they remember it when they need your product or service. For instance, think of a brand like Nike. You don't need to see the word "Nike" to know it's Nike—just seeing the iconic swoosh instantly identifies the brand. This level of recognition is built through consistent use of symbols across all touchpoints.

Why It Matters:
The more people recognize your brand, the more likely they are to choose you when it comes time to make a purchasing decision. Strong brand recognition also helps distinguish your brand from competitors in a crowded

marketplace, making it easier for customers to recall your products or services.

3. Increases Perceived Professionalism and Credibility

Brands that maintain consistency in their symbols across all platforms appear more professional and credible. Consistent branding signals that you take your business seriously and pay attention to detail. It shows that your brand is organized, deliberate, and reliable—key factors that customers consider when choosing who to do business with. Imagine receiving an email from a company with mismatched fonts, logos, or color schemes that don't align with what you saw on their website or social media. It would feel disjointed, and you might question the professionalism of the company. On the other hand, a company that maintains consistent symbols across all interactions communicates reliability, instilling confidence in the customer.

Why It Matters:

Inconsistent branding can make even a great business look unprofessional or untrustworthy. When you maintain a consistent brand identity, customers perceive you as credible and reliable, which is vital for standing out in competitive markets.

4. Enhances Emotional Connection with Your Audience

Consistency in symbols reinforces the emotional connection your audience feels with your brand. When customers repeatedly experience the same visuals, logos, and messaging across different channels, it strengthens the emotional associations they have with your brand. Whether it's trust, excitement, or a sense of belonging, consistency helps deepen that emotional connection over time. For example, customers may associate a specific color with feelings of calm or excitement, and if your brand's color palette remains consistent, it continuously reinforces that emotional connection. Over time, these emotions become linked to your brand, helping foster loyalty.

Why It Matters:
Brands that maintain a consistent visual identity create stronger emotional ties with their audience. This emotional connection builds long-term loyalty, ensuring customers keep coming back and even recommending your brand to others.

Real-World Example: Glossier – Mastering Consistency in Symbols
Glossier, a beauty brand that disrupted the industry with its digital-first, customer-focused approach, has built its success on the strength of consistent branding across all platforms. From its packaging to its social media presence, Glossier has created a visual language that is instantly recognizable, even to those who haven't purchased its products.

1. The Iconic Pink Bubble Packaging
Glossier's pink bubble packaging has become an integral part of its brand identity. Every product arrives in the signature pink pouch, and this packaging has become a symbol of the brand's minimalist, customer-friendly approach. The pink pouch isn't just practical; it's a symbol that Glossier customers have come to love and expect.

This consistency in packaging reinforces Glossier's brand identity across multiple touchpoints, from the moment customers order online to the unboxing experience at home. The pink pouch has become such an iconic symbol that customers often share it on social media, contributing to the brand's recognition.

2. A Minimalist Logo with a Consistent Color Palette

Glossier's logo—a clean, minimalist wordmark—has remained consistent across all channels. The brand uses a soft, monochromatic color palette (primarily soft pinks and whites) that reflects its modern, no-frills approach to beauty. Whether on Instagram, their website, or in-store, Glossier's consistent use of this color palette and minimalist logo ensures that the brand's look is unmistakable.

This subtle but effective consistency is key to Glossier's success. While other beauty brands may use bold, complex logos or bright, flashy colors, Glossier's minimalism is what sets it apart. The simplicity of their logo and color scheme aligns with their "skin first, makeup second" philosophy, creating a cohesive brand identity that their audience connects with.

3. Social Media as a Visual Extension of the Brand

Glossier's social media channels, particularly Instagram, play a significant role in maintaining brand consistency. Their feed is curated with user-generated content, product shots, and lifestyle imagery, all adhering to the brand's clean, minimalist aesthetic. The brand's signature soft pinks and whites are ever-present in their Instagram posts, creating a seamless transition between Glossier's social media presence and its website and product packaging.

By maintaining this level of visual consistency, Glossier has built a community of loyal customers who not only buy their products but actively engage with the brand online. Every Instagram post or ad feels unmistakably like Glossier, whether it's a close-up of a new product or a photo of a customer using their skincare routine.

4. A Consistent Tone of Voice and Messaging
Beyond visuals, Glossier's tone of voice remains consistent across all platforms. Their messaging is always friendly, conversational, and inclusive, reflecting their commitment to making beauty approachable and fun. Whether it's an Instagram caption, a product description on their website, or an email newsletter, Glossier's tone invites customers to feel like they're part of a community.

By aligning their tone of voice with their minimalist symbols and visuals, Glossier creates a cohesive brand experience. This consistency in both visuals and messaging ensures that customers always know what to expect when they interact with the brand, whether online or in-store.

The Impact of Glossier's Consistency
The consistency in Glossier's symbols—its minimalist logo, soft pink packaging, clean typography, and cohesive color palette—has helped the brand build a strong identity that is instantly recognizable across all channels. Customers don't just buy Glossier products; they buy into the brand's aesthetic, values, and community. Every touchpoint, from unboxing a product to scrolling through Instagram, reinforces the same visual and emotional experience.

Why Glossier's Consistency Works:
- Builds Recognition: Glossier's pink bubble wrap, minimalist logo, and soft color palette make the brand instantly recognizable.
- Creates a Sense of Belonging: Consistent branding across platforms helps foster a sense of community, making customers feel like they're part of the "Glossier family."
- Establishes Trust: By delivering a consistent brand experience, Glossier builds trust with its audience, who know exactly what to expect from the brand every time.

Author's Insight
Glossier's success is a testament to the power of consistent symbols. Their brand stands out because they have committed to a clear visual identity that remains true across all platforms. Every touchpoint feels familiar and aligned, making their customers feel confident in their choice.

Glossier's journey highlights the importance of using symbols consistently to reinforce brand identity and build trust with your audience. Whether it's the soft pink packaging, minimalist logo, or carefully curated Instagram feed, each symbol works together to create a unified and memorable brand experience. When your symbols are used consistently across all channels, they strengthen brand recognition, build trust, and establish a sense of professionalism.

Incorporating consistent symbols into your branding isn't just about creating pretty visuals—it's about ensuring that your audience has the same emotional experience with your brand, no matter where they encounter it. When done right, symbols become the anchors of your brand, helping you foster deeper connections with your audience and drive long-term loyalty.

Author's Insight
Consistency doesn't stifle creativity—it amplifies it. When your brand's symbols are consistent, you create a reliable experience that customers can count on, and that reliability is what keeps them coming back.

Creating a Brand Style Guide to Ensure Consistency

To maintain consistent use of your brand's symbols across multiple channels, you need a **brand style guide**. A brand style guide is a document that serves as the blueprint for your brand's visual and messaging standards. It ensures that everyone involved in creating content—whether it's your internal team, freelancers, or external agencies—follows the same rules when using your symbols.

A well-defined style guide is essential for preventing fragmentation in your branding efforts, especially as your business scales and more people contribute to your marketing or content creation.

Key Elements of a Brand Style Guide:
- √ **Logo Guidelines:** Define how and where your logo can be used, including size specifications, placement, and any variations for different platforms (such as a simplified version for small screens).
- √ **Color Palette:** List the exact colors associated with your brand, including hex codes, RGB, and CMYK

values. This ensures your colors are consistent whether in digital media, print, or packaging.

√ **Typography:** Establish the fonts used for headlines, body text, and other content. Specify font sizes and spacing guidelines to create consistency in how your text looks across platforms.

√ **Imagery and Photography:** Define the types of images that align with your brand's style—whether it's lifestyle photos, product shots, or minimalist imagery. Include guidelines on how photos should be edited (e.g., color correction, filters) to maintain a cohesive look.

√ **Tone of Voice:** Your brand's personality should come through in written content. Define whether your brand is formal, conversational, playful, or authoritative, and give examples of how this tone should be applied across different platforms.

√ **Messaging and Key Phrases:** Highlight the core messages and value propositions your brand communicates. Include any key phrases, taglines, or slogans that should be consistently used across all channels.

How to Create a Brand Style Guide:

√ **Start with Your Brand's Purpose:** Review your brand's mission, vision, and values to ensure your style guide reflects the personality and message you want to convey.

√ **Define Your Visual Identity:** Clearly outline your logo usage, color palette, fonts, and image guidelines.

√ **Establish Your Tone of Voice:** Define how your brand communicates in writing and give specific examples of how this tone should be applied across platforms.

√ **Make It Accessible:** Ensure that your style guide is easily accessible to everyone who creates content for your brand, from designers to social media managers.

Real-World Example: Glossier's Brand Style Guide
Glossier's brand style guide is a masterclass in consistency. The guide meticulously details every aspect of the brand's identity, from the precise shade of pink used in packaging to the clean, minimalist aesthetic that defines its product imagery. The guide also includes strict rules on how the brand's logo is applied across different media, ensuring that Glossier's visuals remain cohesive no matter where they appear. This level of detail ensures that the brand experience is always unmistakably Glossier, reinforcing the brand's identity at every touchpoint.

Author's Insight
A brand style guide isn't just for designers—it's for everyone who represents your brand. It's the key to ensuring that no matter who's creating content, your brand identity stays consistent and true to its core.

Using Automation Tools for Brand Consistency
As your brand expands across multiple channels, maintaining consistency manually can become challenging. This is where **automation tools** come in. These tools help streamline your brand's content creation, scheduling, and management processes, ensuring that your symbols—your logos, colors, and messaging—stay consistent without constant oversight.

Automation tools are essential for keeping your brand on track, especially if you're managing content across platforms like Instagram, Facebook, Twitter, LinkedIn, and email newsletters.

Automation tools help ensure that the right message is delivered at the right time, while maintaining brand consistency. They reduce the risk of mistakes, prevent inconsistent branding, and free up time for your team to focus on higher-level strategy.

Top Automation Tools for Brand Consistency:

√ **Buffer:** A social media management tool that allows you to schedule posts across multiple social platforms (like Instagram, Facebook, and Twitter) while maintaining consistent messaging and visuals. You can preview posts to ensure that logos, colors, and tones stay aligned.

√ **Hootsuite:** This tool enables you to manage and schedule content across multiple channels, offering additional features like analytics and collaboration tools. It's perfect for larger teams that need to coordinate content while keeping brand symbols consistent.

√ **Canva:** Canva is a user-friendly design platform that allows you to create branded content consistently. You can save your brand's colors, fonts, and logos, ensuring that every visual adheres to your style guide. Canva's templates make it easy to design consistent visuals for social media, presentations, and more.

√ **Trello:** For teams collaborating on content creation, Trello organizes projects into boards, ensuring that tasks are aligned with your brand's guidelines. Trello helps track progress and ensures that everyone adheres to the brand's style.

√ **Mailchimp:** When it comes to email marketing, Mailchimp lets you create branded email templates and automate campaigns, ensuring that your email newsletters reflect your brand's visuals and messaging every time.

How to Use Automation Tools Effectively:
√ **Schedule Content in Advance:** Use tools like Buffer or Hootsuite to schedule posts ahead of time, ensuring that your visuals and messages are consistent across all platforms.
√ **Set Brand Guidelines in Design Tools:** Canva allows you to store your brand's visual assets, so every design you create is consistent.
√ **Collaborate Seamlessly:** Use tools like Trello to keep track of tasks and ensure that your team stays aligned with your brand's visual and messaging standards.

Author's Insight
Automation isn't just about saving time—it's about maintaining consistency at scale. These tools allow you to focus on the bigger picture while ensuring that every customer interaction reinforces your brand's identity.

Maintaining Consistency Across Top Platforms
Consistency doesn't just happen in one place—it needs to be maintained across every platform where your brand

appears. From social media to email marketing, your symbols should align to create a seamless brand experience no matter where your audience interacts with you. Let's look at the top platforms for brand visibility and how to maintain consistency across each:

1. Instagram
- **Why It's Important:** Instagram is a highly visual platform, making it perfect for showcasing your brand's personality and products.
- **How to Maintain Consistency:**
  - √ Use the same filters or editing style for all posts to create a cohesive aesthetic.
  - √ Stick to your brand's color palette and fonts for Stories, posts, and highlight covers.
  - √ Plan your content in advance with tools like Later or Buffer to maintain a consistent posting schedule.

2. Facebook
- **Why It's Important:** Facebook offers a broad user base and is ideal for sharing longer content and building a community.
- **How to Maintain Consistency:**
  - √ Ensure your profile and cover images are branded with your logo and colors.
  - √ Use Facebook's built-in tools to create consistent messaging, such as automated replies for customer inquiries.
  - √ Schedule posts in advance for consistent engagement.

3. LinkedIn
- **Why It's Important:** LinkedIn is key for establishing your brand's professional identity and thought leadership.

- **How to Maintain Consistency:**
  - √ Ensure your logo and cover image align with your professional branding.
  - √ Share content that highlights your expertise, such as case studies and whitepapers.
  - √ Keep your tone consistent across posts and professional outreach.

4. X (formerly Twitter)
- **Why It's Important:** Twitter is great for real-time conversations and engaging with your audience on trending topics.
- **How to Maintain Consistency:**
  - √ Use your brand's logo and consistent imagery for your profile and cover photo.
  - √ Maintain a consistent tone—whether it's witty, informative, or formal.
  - √ Schedule tweets with tools like Buffer to ensure consistent posting.

5. Email Marketing (Mailchimp, etc.)
- **Why It's Important:** Email remains one of the most direct ways to communicate with your audience.
- **How to Maintain Consistency:**
  - √ Use branded email templates with your logo, colors, and fonts.
  - √ Ensure that your subject lines and content reflect your brand's tone and personality.
  - √ Schedule newsletters or automated campaigns for consistent engagement.

Author's Insight

No matter which platform you're on, consistency is the glue that holds your brand together. When your symbols—your logo, colors, and voice—are consistent, you create a seamless experience that builds trust and loyalty.

The Power of Consistency in Symbols

Brand consistency is about making sure your symbols—your logo, colors, typography, and messaging—are aligned across all channels. These symbols are the visual and emotional cues that connect your audience to your brand's identity. When used consistently, they become recognizable and trustworthy, reinforcing your brand's values and purpose at every touchpoint.

As you continue to build your brand, remember that consistency in symbols is what helps you create a cohesive experience that resonates with your audience. By creating a brand style guide, using automation tools, and maintaining consistency across platforms, you'll create a brand that not only stands out but builds lasting trust and loyalty.

Author's Insight

Symbols are the language your brand speaks. When used consistently, they become the visual markers of trust, familiarity, and identity that your customers come to recognize and rely on. Get them right, and you've built the foundation for a brand that's both memorable and unshakeable.

BRAND CONSISTENCY AUDIT CHECKLIST: ENSURING ALIGNMENT ACROSS ALL CHANNELS

Use this checklist to audit your current branding efforts and ensure your messaging, visuals, and customer interactions are consistent and aligned across every platform. This will help you build a cohesive, trustworthy, and memorable brand experience.

1. Visual Identity

√ **Logo Usage**
- ☐ Is your logo the same across all platforms (website, social media, email)?
- ☐ Are there clear guidelines for logo placement, size, and color variations?
- ☐ Is the logo recognizable and correctly used on both digital and print materials?

√ **Color Palette**
- ☐ Are your brand colors consistent across all media (website, social posts, packaging, etc.)?
- ☐ Do you use the exact color codes (HEX, RGB, CMYK) for digital and print formats?
- ☐ Is your color palette applied to all branded materials, from ads to product packaging?

√ **Typography**
- ☐ Are you using the same fonts across your website, social media, email, and printed materials?
- ☐ Are font sizes and styles consistent in headings, body text, and CTAs?
- ☐ Do your font choices reflect your brand's personality and tone?

2. Brand Messaging
√ Taglines and Slogans
- ☐ Is your tagline or slogan used consistently in your marketing materials and online profiles?
- ☐ Does your slogan reflect your brand's mission, values, and tone?

√ Core Message
- ☐ Are the key benefits and values of your brand communicated consistently across all platforms?
- ☐ Are your marketing campaigns, social media posts, and advertisements delivering a unified message?
- ☐ Do your emails, blogs, and website reflect the same core message as your promotional materials?

√ Tone of Voice
- ☐ Is your brand's tone of voice (casual, professional, playful, etc.) the same across social media, website copy, and customer support interactions?
- ☐ Is the language used in customer emails, social media captions, and blog posts consistent?
- ☐ Are your tone and messaging appropriate for your target audience on all channels?

3. Customer Experience & Interaction
√ Customer Service
- ☐ Are customer service interactions aligned with your brand's values and tone?

- ☐ Are your response times and solutions consistent across all touchpoints (email, social media, chat)?
- ☐ Is customer support trained to reflect the brand's messaging in all communications?

√ **Social Media Engagement**
- ☐ Is your engagement with customers on social media (comments, messages, replies) reflective of your brand's tone and values?
- ☐ Are you using consistent messaging when responding to feedback or questions across all platforms?
- ☐ Is your content strategy consistent in how you present your brand on social media?

√ **Website & E-commerce**
- ☐ Does your website design (layout, fonts, colors) match your overall brand identity?
- ☐ Is your product or service messaging clear and aligned with what's communicated on other platforms?
- ☐ Are the customer interactions on your website (chatbots, contact forms, etc.) consistent with your brand's tone and professionalism?

4. Marketing and Campaigns
√ **Advertisements**
- ☐ Do your online ads (Google, Facebook, Instagram) match the messaging and visuals on your website and social media?

    ☐ Is the tone and style of your paid campaigns aligned with your overall brand identity?

√ **Email Marketing**
- ☐ Are your email templates and designs consistent with your website and social platforms?
- ☐ Is the language used in your newsletters, promotions, and follow-up emails in line with your brand tone?

√ **Packaging & Offline Materials**
- ☐ Are your product packaging and printed materials (business cards, brochures) aligned with your digital branding?
- ☐ Is your brand's look and feel consistent between offline and online interactions?

5. Monitoring and Adaptation

√ **Brand Guidelines**
- ☐ Do you have a documented **brand style guide** that outlines logo usage, colors, fonts, and messaging?

√ **Consistency Check**
- ☐ Are you regularly reviewing your brand's messaging/visuals across all platforms?
- ☐ Are there any platforms/touchpoints where your brand looks or feels inconsistent?

√ **Adaptation & Updates**
- ○ Are you monitoring and adapting your brand's visuals or messaging to suit new platforms?

Hey, this is Karee ♥

Thank you for taking the time to dive into this book and explore the journey of building a powerful, authentic brand. I truly hope that the insights, strategies, and stories shared within these pages have inspired you to take bold steps in shaping your brand and making your vision a reality.

Your feedback means the world to me. If this book brought you value or sparked new ideas, I'd be incredibly grateful if you could take a moment to leave a review on Amazon. Your review not only helps me reach more entrepreneurs, creators, and business owners but also supports others in finding the guidance they need to build the brand they've always dreamed of.

Thank you for being part of this journey, and I can't wait to see the incredible brands you create!

Karee

CHAPTER 6: BUILDING A BRAND THAT BECOMES ESSENTIAL

"When you buy an Apple product, you aren't just buying a computer or a phone. You are buying into the idea that technology can empower creativity, that it can be simple yet groundbreaking and that it will integrate seamlessly into your life. And most importantly, you are buying into a sense of identity—Apple isn't for everyone, it's for those who dare to think different."

This chapter explores how to **see your brand grow strong by becoming part of your customer's routine**. We'll delve into how brands like Glossier and others have done this, and how you can develop and sustain that same connection by ensuring your brand is woven into the fabric of your customers' daily lives.

Why Routines Are Vital for Brand Longevity
When customers incorporate your brand into their daily routines, it becomes a trusted companion. A brand that customers use day after day creates familiarity and, more

importantly, **dependence.** Brands that solve problems consistently position themselves as not just a product, but a **lifestyle choice.**

Think about how certain brands have become a natural part of daily routines—whether it's reaching for your phone in the morning (Apple), applying skincare (Glossier), or grabbing a quick coffee on the go (Starbucks). These brands have succeeded because they are solving problems or enhancing their customers' lives in ways that are simple, efficient, and reliable. When your brand becomes routine, it builds customer loyalty because it's seen as essential rather than optional.

> **Author's Insight**
> Strong brands don't just show up when needed—they become so intertwined with the customer's life that they're used without thinking. They're part of the fabric of daily living.

The Key to Embedding Your Brand in Daily Routines
1. Solve a Core Problem Consistently
The most important aspect of embedding your brand into your customers' daily routines is solving a key problem **reliably.** If your product or service offers a solution that makes life easier, faster, or better, customers will naturally turn to it time and time again. By being a dependable problem-solver, you become their go-to brand.

This is Branding Example: Glossier
Glossier, the skincare and beauty brand, has mastered the art of solving a core problem for its audience—**simple, effective beauty routines.** Glossier's ethos of "skin first,

makeup second" aligns perfectly with its audience's desire for products that enhance natural beauty without being overly complicated. Glossier's products like their **Milky Jelly Cleanser** or **Balm Dotcom** are staples in many morning and evening skincare routines because they solve everyday beauty needs—hydration, cleanliness, and protection—in an easy-to-use, effective way.

By consistently solving the problem of accessible skincare and beauty, Glossier has embedded itself into the daily rituals of its customers.

How to Implement This Strategy:

√ **Identify Your Core Problem:** Ask yourself, "What issue does my brand solve for my customers every day?" Understanding this core problem allows you to focus on delivering consistent solutions.

√ **Build Reliability:** Ensure your product or service delivers on its promise consistently. Reliability is what makes customers reach for your brand without hesitation.

2. Create Products or Services that Fit Seamlessly into Daily Life

To truly integrate into your customer's routine, your product or service should **fit effortlessly** into their day. It should be easy to use, accessible, and feel like a natural part of their existing habits. When your brand fits into their daily rhythm, it reduces friction and increases the likelihood of long-term loyalty.

This is Branding Example: Peloton
Peloton, the fitness brand, has become part of daily routines for millions of people by making at-home

workouts accessible, engaging, and effective. The key to Peloton's success is that it fits seamlessly into the customer's routine—whether they're squeezing in a 20-minute ride before work or a full 45-minute workout on the weekend. Peloton's integration with their customers' daily lives is further reinforced by features like live classes, on-demand workouts, and the ability to track progress over time. It's easy for customers to build Peloton into their fitness routines without disrupting their daily lives.

How to Implement This Strategy:
- √ **Ease of Use:** Make sure your product or service can be easily integrated into your customers' schedules. If it's complicated or difficult to use, it will be abandoned quickly.
- √ **Offer Flexibility:** Ensure that your product or service offers flexibility in how it's used so that it can adapt to different aspects of your customers' routines.

3. Build Emotional Connections Through Routines
Brands that embed themselves into routines are not just solving functional problems; they also **create emotional connections**. Over time, your product or service can become part of a ritual or habit that brings comfort, confidence, or even joy. When customers emotionally connect with your brand in their daily life, they're more likely to remain loyal.

This is Branding Example: Starbucks
For many, the act of grabbing a cup of coffee from Starbucks isn't just about caffeine—it's a ritual that brings a sense of comfort and routine. The familiarity of ordering a favorite drink, the sound of the barista calling your name,

and the consistent experience of the brand become emotionally charged moments that are woven into the fabric of daily life. Starbucks has made itself an essential part of many customers' routines because it delivers both a functional (caffeine) and emotional (comfort) experience.

How to Implement This Strategy:
- √ **Create Rituals:** Find ways to make your brand part of a customer's daily ritual. This could be through the use of packaging, messaging, or customer interactions that reinforce positive emotions.
- √ **Emphasize Experience:** Don't just solve a problem—create an experience. Whether it's the unboxing of your product or the satisfaction of using it, ensure the emotional aspect of the routine is part of your brand.

Staying Relevant in a Changing World: Adapting Without Losing Your Brand's Core
In a world where technology advances rapidly, customer preferences shift, and new competitors emerge regularly, staying relevant is crucial to your brand's longevity. The most successful brands aren't just those that adapt—they're the ones that evolve while staying true to their **core identity**. Staying relevant means continually meeting your customers' needs, keeping up with trends, and positioning yourself to thrive in changing environments without losing what makes your brand unique.

In this section, we'll explore the importance of adaptability, how to evolve your brand offerings, and ways to stay relevant in a constantly changing market while preserving your brand's core identity. The goal is to ensure that your brand remains a vital part of your customers' lives no matter how the world shifts around them.

Why Staying Relevant Is Key to Long-Term Success

The marketplace is constantly evolving. What worked a few years ago—or even a few months ago—might not be enough to keep your brand top-of-mind today. Advances in technology, changes in customer behavior, and the rise of new competitors can disrupt the status quo, making it essential for brands to stay flexible. But staying relevant doesn't mean completely reinventing your brand every time a new trend emerges. Instead, it means adapting strategically while staying true to your core values.

Why Staying Relevant Matters:
- √ **Evolving Customer Expectations:** Today's customers expect more than just a product or service—they want **experiences** that align with their changing lifestyles, values, and needs. If your brand fails to keep pace with these shifts, you risk becoming outdated or irrelevant.
- √ **Technological Advances:** Innovations such as AI, mobile technology, and digital platforms continuously reshape how customers interact with brands. To remain relevant, businesses must integrate new technologies that enhance the customer experience while keeping their brand values intact.
- √ **Competitive Pressure:** As new brands emerge and markets become more saturated, it's crucial to differentiate your brand by adapting to the competitive landscape. Failing to innovate or evolve can lead to competitors outpacing you in

terms of customer engagement, product offerings, and overall relevance.

Author's Insight
Relevance isn't about chasing every trend—it's about strategically adapting to the changes that matter most to your customers. Stay true to your core but be flexible enough to evolve with the world around you.

Staying Relevant Without Losing Your Core Identity
1. Monitor Market Trends and Customer Preferences
The first step in staying relevant is **keeping a finger on the pulse** of industry trends and understanding how customer preferences are changing. Whether it's through social listening, data analytics, or customer feedback, consistently gather insights that will help you stay informed about shifts in your market.

How to Monitor Trends:
- √ **Leverage Social Media and Industry Reports**: Social media is a powerful tool for keeping track of emerging trends and understanding what's resonating with your audience. Use platforms like Instagram, TikTok, and Twitter to see what your customers are talking about. Subscribe to industry reports and publications that provide insights into broader market movements.
- √ **Conduct Regular Surveys and Feedback**: Regularly ask your customers for feedback through surveys, reviews, and polls. This not only helps you understand what they value but also identifies areas for improvement. A brand that listens to its audience stays ahead of their changing needs.

√ **Stay Aware of Competitor Movements:** Keep an eye on how your competitors are responding to market changes. While you don't need to follow their lead, understanding their approach can help you position your brand uniquely and highlight your strengths.

This is Branding Example: Glossier
Glossier has successfully stayed relevant in the ever-evolving beauty industry by staying in tune with customer preferences and industry trends. Known for their minimalist skincare and beauty products, Glossier regularly engages with their community on social media to gather feedback and understand what their customers want. When they noticed a growing trend toward sustainability, they adapted by creating more eco-friendly packaging and products, aligning with their customers' values while staying true to their core identity of simplicity and accessibility.

2. Innovate Within Your Space
Innovation is key to remaining relevant, but it doesn't mean you need to reinvent your brand entirely. Instead, focus on **innovating within your niche**, using your brand's strengths as a foundation for new products, services, or experiences. Brands that continually find ways to innovate are the ones that not only survive but thrive as market conditions shift.

How to Innovate While Staying True to Your Brand:
√ **Introduce New Products or Services:** Evolve your product offerings to align with current customer needs. These innovations should still reflect your brand's core mission and values. For example,

when **Peloton** noticed that customers were looking for more than just indoor cycling classes, they expanded their offerings to include strength training, yoga, and even meditation. This allowed them to stay relevant without straying from their core mission of accessible fitness.

√ **Incorporate New Technologies:** Technology can enhance the customer experience in ways that keep your brand relevant. For example, adding mobile apps, virtual reality (VR), or AI-powered customer service can elevate your offerings. **Nike** has embraced innovation by integrating their fitness products with technology, such as the Nike Run Club app, which offers personalized coaching and progress tracking, keeping Nike products integrated into their customers' fitness routines.

√ **Adapt Your Marketing Strategy:** In today's digital age, adapting your marketing strategy is essential. Shift your focus to where your customers spend the most time—whether that's on social media, through influencer marketing, or using video content. Brands like **Netflix** have mastered the art of evolving their marketing strategies, constantly experimenting with new forms of digital advertising, original content, and personalized recommendations to keep users engaged.

Author's Insight

Innovation isn't about changing who you are—it's about pushing your brand forward while holding onto what makes you unique. Evolve thoughtfully, and your audience will follow you into the future.

---

3. Embrace New Technologies and Platforms

Technology is constantly changing the way consumers interact with brands, and it's crucial to keep pace. From AI to automation and social media platforms, embracing new technologies can improve the customer experience and keep your brand at the forefront of your industry.

How to Leverage Technology to Stay Relevant:

- √ **Incorporate AI and Automation:** AI-powered tools can help brands stay relevant by improving personalization, customer service, and engagement. For example, brands like **Sephora** have adopted AI-driven chatbots to offer personalized beauty recommendations based on customers' preferences, creating a more tailored and efficient shopping experience.
- √ **Adapt to New Platforms:** As social media platforms evolve brands must adapt to where their customers spend time. For instance, **TikTok** became a massive platform for reaching Gen Z and younger audiences, and brands like Chipotle have used it successfully for viral marketing campaigns. If your target audience is shifting to new platforms, follow them and find ways to engage effectively on those channels.
- √ **Enhance the Digital Experience:** The rise of e-commerce and mobile-first interactions means that your website, app, and digital tools need to be seamless and user-friendly. **Amazon** remains a leader in e-commerce because they continuously optimize their user experience with features like one-click purchasing, or even personalized recommendations, and voice-enabled shopping via Alexa.

This is Branding Example: Zoom

Zoom's rapid rise during the COVID-19 pandemic is an example of how embracing technology at the right time can position a brand as essential. As remote work and virtual communication became the new normal, Zoom quickly adapted to become a reliable tool for both personal and professional use. Their ability to scale and introduce features like virtual backgrounds, breakout rooms, and improved security allowed them to stay relevant and become part of people's daily routines.

4. Evolve Your Brand Offerings Without Losing Your Core Identity

While staying relevant requires adaptation, it's equally important to maintain the **core essence** of your brand. Your brand's mission, vision, and values should remain constant, even as you introduce new products, services, or marketing strategies. Consistency in these areas builds trust and loyalty, ensuring that your customers know what your brand stands for no matter how much the world changes.

How to Maintain Your Core Identity:

√ **Stay True to Your Brand's Purpose:** As you evolve, regularly check in on your brand's mission and values to ensure that everything you do aligns with your core purpose. When you innovate, ask yourself: "Does this still represent what our brand stands for?" For example, **Patagonia** consistently stays true to its environmental values, even as they expand their product line. Whether through sustainable materials or their advocacy for climate change, Patagonia remains committed to its core mission of protecting the planet.

√ **Reinforce Your Brand Values in Marketing:** As you evolve, ensure that your marketing campaigns and messaging still reflect your core values. Use storytelling to remind your audience of what your brand stands for, especially during times of change or growth. **Ben & Jerry's** consistently reinforces their commitment to social justice and environmental activism, even as they introduce new flavors and expand globally. This alignment with their core values keeps them relevant and trusted by their audience.

√ **Use Consistent Visual and Emotional Branding:** While evolving your product or service, maintain consistency in your brand's visuals and tone. Whether through your logo, color palette, or messaging style, this continuity reinforces your identity even as you expand. **Apple**, for example, continues to innovate its product line with every new iPhone or MacBook, yet their brand's minimalist aesthetic and commitment to user experience remain the same.

Author's Insight

Adapting to change doesn't mean losing sight of who you are. Your brand's mission is the anchor that keeps you grounded as you explore new opportunities and evolve. Stay consistent in your values, and you'll build trust, even as you innovate.

Balancing Adaptability and Consistency for Relevance

Staying relevant in a changing world requires a delicate balance between **adaptability** and **consistency**. Brands that evolve to meet new customer needs, adopt emerging technologies, and innovate their offerings will remain top-of-mind in their industry.

However, true success comes from doing this while maintaining a strong connection to your brand's core identity. By continually listening to your customers, staying aware of market trends, and evolving your product or service offerings, you can ensure your brand remains a part of your customers' lives—no matter how the world changes.

> **Author's Insight**
> Brands that stand the test of time are those that adapt thoughtfully and strategically. Embrace change, but always remember who you are at the core. Stay flexible, stay relevant, but never lose sight of what makes your brand special.

Steps to Embed Your Brand in Daily Routines

Embedding your brand into your customer's daily routines is one of the most powerful ways to build long-term loyalty and ensure your brand's relevance. When customers naturally integrate your product or service into their day-to-day lives, you become indispensable—a part of their habitual behavior, something they rely on. To achieve this, your brand must consistently solve a problem, provide ease of use, adapt to changing needs, and build emotional connections. Let's explore each of these steps in greater detail.

1. Be a Problem-Solver: Always Address a Core Need

The foundation of embedding your brand into a daily routine is solving a real, **consistent problem** that your customers face. People gravitate toward brands that offer solutions to their everyday challenges, whether it's providing convenience, saving time, improving health, or making life easier. If your brand can do this reliably, customers will return to it again and again, making it an essential part of their routine.

How to Become a Problem-Solver:

√ **Identify Your Audience's Key Pain Points:** This could start with conducting customer research to uncover the specific problems your product or service addresses. You can accomplish this through surveys, reviews, or focus groups. Understanding what challenges your customers face will allow you to position your brand as the reliable solution.

√ **Provide Consistent Solutions:** Make sure your product or service is dependable. If it solves the problem well every time, your customers will come to depend on it. Think of a product like **Slack**, the business communication platform. Slack has embedded itself into the daily routines of teams by providing a reliable solution for workplace collaboration and communication. The consistent performance of the platform makes it indispensable for companies.

√ **Deliver Ongoing Value:** A one-time solution is not enough. Ensure that your product or service offers **ongoing** value, so customers have a reason to come back every day. For example, Headspace, a meditation app, provides daily meditation sessions that help users relieve stress and improve mental clarity. This continuous value makes it easy for customers to make Headspace part of their daily mental wellness routine.

Author's Insight
Brands that thrive don't just show up once—they're there day after day, helping their customers solve problems in small but meaningful ways. If you're consistently part of their solution, you're on the path to becoming a habit.

---

2. Create Simplicity and Ease of Use: Make It Effortless
To become part of a daily routine, your product or service needs to be **easy to use** and **seamless to integrate** into the customer's day. People are busy, and they don't want to waste time figuring out complicated processes. The easier you make it for your customers to engage with your brand, the more likely they are to stick with it.

How to Create Ease of Use:
√ **Streamline the User Experience:** Whether it's the layout of your app, the design of your product packaging, or the checkout process on your website, ensure that every interaction is simple and intuitive. For example, **Uber** revolutionized transportation by making it incredibly easy to book a ride. The app is simple, efficient, and frictionless, making it easy for users to integrate into their routines for commuting or getting around town.
√ **Offer Quick and Convenient Access:** Ensure that your product or service is easily accessible. This could mean being available on multiple devices, offering fast delivery, or making your service available 24/7. For example, **Amazon** has mastered ease of use with its **one-click purchasing** feature and fast delivery services

like **Prime**, which ensure that customers can quickly get the products they need, making Amazon a go-to solution for daily shopping needs.

√ **Minimize the Effort to Use Your Product:** Reduce the steps needed for customers to use your product or service. The fewer obstacles between them and the solution, the more likely they are to incorporate it into their routine. **Spotify** has done this by providing personalized playlists like "Discover Weekly" and "Daily Mix," offering music that customers love without them needing to search for it. The simplicity of having curated content delivered automatically encourages users to return to the platform daily.

Author's Insight

People value their time—if your brand fits effortlessly into their lives, they'll return to you again and again. Make their experience frictionless, and you'll find a place in their daily routine.

---

3. Evolve with Customers' Changing Needs

As customer preferences shift, technology evolves, and industries change, your brand needs to stay **flexible** and **adapt** to remain relevant. Brands that are rigid risk losing their place in their customers' routines as competitors offer more relevant or modern solutions. To stay embedded in daily life, your brand must evolve without losing its core identity.

How to Stay Adaptable:

√ **Regularly Gather Customer Feedback:** Continuously ask for feedback from your customers to understand how your product fits into their routine. This will help you spot areas for improvement or new features that could make their lives even easier. For example, **Netflix** frequently collects data on viewing habits, using it to tailor content suggestions and improve the user experience. This ongoing adaptation ensures that Netflix remains a staple in daily entertainment routines.

√ **Embrace New Technologies and Trends:** Keep up with industry trends and technological advancements to ensure your product or service stays relevant. Brands that are quick to adopt new platforms or channels (like mobile apps, voice search, or social media) can stay top-of-mind for customers. For instance, **Nike** has successfully integrated technology with its fitness gear by developing the **Nike Training Club** app, which offers users a convenient way to work out from home. This has become an integral part of many users' daily fitness routines.

√ **Evolve Your Offerings Based on Customer Needs:** Be willing to change your product or service offering if your customers' needs evolve. By staying flexible and responsive, your brand will remain essential even as markets change. A great example is **Zoom**, which evolved from a niche business tool to a globally recognized platform during the COVID-19 pandemic. As remote work and virtual events became a new daily routine for many people, Zoom adapted to become an integral part of both personal and professional life.

4. Build Emotional Connections: Make Your Brand a Ritual

When a brand taps into not just functional needs but **emotional ones**, it becomes more than just a product—it becomes a part of the customer's life they look forward to using. Whether it's the sense of accomplishment from finishing a task or the calm from starting a meditation session, emotional connections turn everyday actions into **rituals**.

How to Build Emotional Connections:

√ **Create Meaningful Rituals:** Think about how your brand can be tied to positive moments in your customers' day. These can be small but meaningful rituals that add joy, convenience, or satisfaction to their routine. **Apple,** for example, has made the act of unboxing a new product a deeply emotional experience. The sleek packaging, minimalistic design, and ease of setup create a sense of excitement and accomplishment, turning the unboxing itself into a ritual for Apple fans.

√ **Focus on Consistency and Quality:** Emotional connections are built on trust, and trust comes from consistently delivering a great experience. Brands like **Starbucks** create emotional ties by providing customers with the same comforting experience every time they visit, making that daily cup of coffee feel like a small but important part of the customer's day.

√ **Tell Stories that Resonate:** Use storytelling in your brand messaging that aligns with your customers' values and emotions. Brands that tell meaningful stories can create deeper emotional connections with their audience. **TOMS**, for example, uses storytelling to emphasize its "One for One" mission—every purchase helps someone in need. This emotional connection makes customers feel like they're making a difference every time they buy from TOMS, embedding the brand into their routine as a purposeful choice.

Author's Insight

Emotions are powerful drivers of behavior. When you create a brand that makes customers feel good—whether it's through a sense of comfort, accomplishment, or purpose—you're no longer just a product or service. You're a daily ritual they don't want to skip.

Embedding your brand into your customers' daily routines means more than just being useful—it means being essential. By solving a core problem, making your brand effortless to use, staying adaptable to change, and building emotional connections, you can transform your brand from a transactional experience to a habitual one. When customers rely on you daily, your brand becomes part of their lifestyle, securing long-term loyalty and growth.

Author's Insight
Brands that last are brands that become part of the daily rhythm. They don't just sell—they serve, support, and enhance their customers' lives. Make your brand something your customers can't imagine living without, and you'll be building a legacy.

CHAPTER 7: BUILDING A CULT BRAND BY DEFINING YOUR BRAND ETHOS – THE POWER OF OPPONENTS

"To build a cult brand, it's not enough to stand for something—you must stand against something. Opposition sharpens your identity, unites your tribe, and turns customers into believers."

One of the most powerful forces in branding comes from the **opponents** you define and position your brand against. The strongest brands don't just stand for something—they stand **against** something. They take a clear stance, drawing a line between themselves and everything they're not. This opposition creates a sharp contrast that resonates deeply with the right audience, solidifying loyalty and driving a passionate, almost cult-like following.

In this chapter, we'll explore how identifying and defining your opponents can help you craft a compelling **brand**

ethos and messaging that speaks to your ideal audience. By clearly stating what you stand for—and what you stand against—you can attract like-minded customers, differentiate yourself from competitors, and build a brand that inspires loyalty and devotion. We'll dive into real-world examples of brands that have mastered this approach and provide actionable insights to help you do the same.

The Importance of Defining Opponents in Branding
In branding, an opponent doesn't necessarily have to be a direct competitor. Instead, it can be any concept, belief, or status quo that your brand rejects. By defining what your brand opposes, you create a clearer identity and position yourself as the antidote to a problem or frustration your audience faces. This contrast makes your brand more **memorable**, **relatable**, and emotionally charged.

Defining opponents helps you:
- √ **Clarify Your Brand Ethos:** By clearly stating what you stand against, you sharpen what you stand for. This creates a well-defined brand ethos, or guiding belief system, that resonates with your audience.
- √ **Differentiate from Competitors:** While many brands may offer similar products or services, not all take a bold stand. Positioning yourself against something sets you apart in a way that goes beyond features and benefits.
- √ **Attract the Right Audience:** Your opponents reflect the beliefs and frustrations of your audience. When you take a strong stance against something your audience rejects, you attract customers who share your values.

√ **Build a Cult-Like Following:** Brands that stand against something often inspire a passionate and loyal fan base. These customers see themselves as part of a movement or community, not just buyers of a product.

Author's Insight
Opposition is a powerful tool in branding. It clarifies your identity and brings like-minded people together. When you draw a line in the sand, you're not just selling a product—you're offering a belief system that people can rally behind.

Step 1: Identifying Your Opponents
The first step in using opponents to build your brand ethos is to identify what your brand stands against. This isn't about picking fights with competitors—it's about understanding the larger **values, practices, or beliefs** that you reject and positioning your brand as the alternative.

Types of Opponents to Consider:
√ **Cultural Opponents:** These are larger societal beliefs, trends, or practices that your brand stands against. For example, **Patagonia** stands against the overconsumption and environmental destruction caused by fast fashion. Their entire brand ethos is built around sustainability, repairable gear, and reducing waste, setting them apart in an industry often driven by trends and disposability.
√ **Industry Opponents:** Sometimes, the status quo in your industry can become an opponent. For

example, **Tesla** positioned itself against the traditional fossil-fuel-powered car industry, standing as a champion for electric vehicles and sustainable energy solutions. This opposition has been key to Tesla's rise as an industry disruptor.

√ **Ideological Opponents:** These are specific belief systems or mindsets that your brand rejects. For instance, **Glossier** stands against the over-complicated, high-maintenance beauty standards set by many traditional makeup brands. Instead, Glossier promotes a minimalist, "skin first" approach, appealing to an audience that values simplicity and authenticity in beauty.

Questions to Ask When Identifying Your Opponents:

√ What frustrations or pain points do our customers face that we can solve?

√ What outdated practices or beliefs does our brand challenge?

√ What industry norms or standards do we reject?

√ How do we want to position ourselves as the antidote to a problem?

This is Branding Example: Oatly

Oatly, the oat milk brand, has positioned itself as a rebellious disruptor in the dairy industry. The company takes a firm stance against traditional dairy consumption, using cheeky and confrontational messaging like "It's like milk, but made for humans." Oatly's bold opposition to dairy has earned them a cult following among consumers looking for plant-based alternatives and a more sustainable way to consume milk. Their marketing campaigns target not just the product but the belief behind it—plant-based diets as a healthier and more environmentally friendly option. By defining their opponent as traditional dairy, Oatly has built a strong ethos that resonates with their eco-conscious audience.

Step 2: Crafting Your Brand Ethos

Once you've defined your opponents, you can start building your **brand ethos** around what you stand for and how you position yourself as the solution. Your brand ethos is the core set of values and principles that guide every aspect of your business—from your messaging and marketing to the way you develop products or services. It's not just what you sell, but the **why** behind it.

Your brand ethos should answer:
- √ What do we believe in?
- √ What are we fighting for?
- √ How do our products or services reflect these beliefs?

By clearly defining these elements, you create a brand that feels authentic, purposeful, and emotionally resonant. Customers are no longer just buying a product—they're buying into a belief system.

How to Build a Strong Brand Ethos:
- √ **Center Around Core Values:** Your brand ethos should be rooted in deeply held values. These values guide everything from your product development to your customer interactions. For example, **Ben & Jerry's** centers its brand ethos around social justice, environmental sustainability, and ethical business practices. These values are reflected not just in their marketing but in their product sourcing, employee policies, and activism.

√ **Create Messaging That Reflects Your Beliefs:** Your brand ethos should come through clearly in your messaging. Use your website, packaging, social media, and advertising to communicate your beliefs consistently. Brands like **Chick-fil-A** have built their ethos around strong Christian values, which are reflected in everything from their customer service to their decision to close on Sundays.

√ **Be Authentic and Transparent:** Customers can tell when a brand is being disingenuous. Your ethos must feel authentic, and your actions should align with your stated beliefs. **Patagonia**, for example, is known for its environmental activism. When they encourage customers to repair or recycle their gear instead of buying new products, it's a genuine reflection of their commitment to sustainability.

This is Branding Example: Allbirds

Allbirds, the sustainable footwear brand, has built its ethos around the principle of creating comfortable shoes while minimizing environmental impact. They oppose wasteful production methods and the overuse of synthetic materials. Instead, Allbirds uses natural materials like wool and eucalyptus, positioning themselves against traditional shoe manufacturers that rely on environmentally harmful processes.

Their ethos of sustainability, simplicity, and innovation has attracted eco-conscious consumers and built a loyal, almost cult-like following. Allbirds' commitment to transparency and environmentally friendly production practices reinforces their brand ethos and strengthens customer loyalty.

Step 3: Messaging for Your Ideal Audience

Once you have a clear brand ethos, the next step is creating messaging that resonates with your **ideal audience**. By using your opponents as a point of differentiation, you can speak directly to the frustrations, values, and desires of your target customers. Messaging is key to building a brand that not only attracts the right audience but also **inspires loyalty** and **emotional engagement**.

How to Develop Messaging that Attracts a Cult Following:

√ **Speak to Your Audience's Pain Points:** Use messaging that highlights what your audience is tired of, frustrated with, or ready to move away from. This could be anything from outdated industry practices to cultural trends that no longer resonate with them. For example, **Dollar Shave Club** targeted customers who were frustrated with expensive, overly complex shaving products sold by major brands like Gillette. Their simple, humorous messaging, paired with affordable pricing, spoke directly to an underserved audience that wanted a better alternative.

√ **Frame Your Brand as the Solution:** Once you've identified what your audience is against, clearly position your brand as the solution. Show how your product or service solves the problem, challenges the status quo, and offers a better alternative. For instance, **Warby Parker positioned itself as a direct-to-consumer** brand that cuts out the middleman, offering stylish, affordable glasses. They stood against the traditional eyewear industry, where consumers were paying excessive prices for basic eyewear.

√ **Use Bold, Polarizing Language:** To attract a passionate following, your messaging needs to be bold. Don't be afraid to be polarizing—brands that play it safe often blend into the noise. Brands like **Supreme** have built cult-like followings by taking strong, unapologetic stances. Supreme's messaging is infused with exclusivity and streetwear culture, creating a sense of belonging for those "in the know" while excluding those who don't fit the brand's ethos.

√ **Leverage Emotional Appeals:** Emotional storytelling helps connect your brand to your audience's values and desires. Use your messaging to evoke emotions like excitement, rebellion, or empowerment. The more your audience feels connected to your brand on an emotional level, the more loyal they will be. **Nike**, for example, doesn't just sell shoes—they sell empowerment, using slogans like "Just Do It" to inspire customers to push their limits.

This is Branding Example: Peloton
Peloton, the home fitness brand, has created a cult following by speaking directly to an audience that feels disconnected from traditional gym experiences. Peloton's messaging focuses on the convenience and personalization of home workouts, but it also speaks to a larger sense of belonging and community. Through their instructors, online classes, and social media presence, Peloton positions itself against the impersonal nature of

traditional gyms and fitness programs. By framing their product as a way to connect, stay fit, and be part of an exclusive community, Peloton has cultivated a passionate, loyal customer base.

Step 4: Building a Cult-Like Following
A **cult brand** is built when your audience becomes emotionally invested in your brand ethos and shares your opposition to the same values or beliefs. These customers are not just buying your product—they are buying into a lifestyle, a movement, or an identity. Cult brands inspire devotion, advocacy, and a sense of community among their customers.

How to Build a Cult Following:
- √ **Create a Strong Sense of Belonging:** Cult brands make their customers feel like they are part of an exclusive community. Whether it's through limited-edition products, members-only access, or loyalty programs, find ways to create exclusivity and a sense of belonging. For example, Supreme creates hype and exclusivity through limited product drops, which fosters a tight-knit community of loyal fans who feel like they're part of something special.

- √ **Foster Community Engagement:** Build spaces where your customers can interact with your brand and each other. This could be through social media, online forums, or in-person events. Brands like **Glossier** have built a community through social media, encouraging customers to share their experiences and create user-generated content. This level of engagement deepens the connection customers   feel   with   the   brand.

√ **Stand for Something Bigger:** Cult brands often stand for something larger than just the product. Align your brand with a bigger mission or purpose that resonates with your audience. **Patagonia** has cultivated a passionate following by aligning its brand with environmental activism. Customers don't just buy Patagonia gear; they feel like they're supporting a larger cause that aligns with their values.

√ **Reward Loyalty:** Create loyalty programs or offer exclusive perks to your most devoted customers. This reinforces the sense of belonging and incentivizes repeat purchases. **Starbucks,** for example, has built a loyal customer base through its **Starbucks Rewards** program, offering exclusive benefits like free drinks, personalized offers, and early access to new products.

Standing for Something, Standing Against Something

By defining your brand ethos and identifying your opponents, you can position your brand as a beacon for customers who share your values. This opposition clarifies your identity, strengthens your message, and builds emotional connections with the right audience. As a result, your brand isn't just selling products—it's building a loyal, passionate following that sees your brand as part of their identity.

Author's Insight

Cult brands aren't built overnight. They're the result of consistently standing for something—and standing against something. When you clearly define your ethos, your opponents, and your audience, you create a brand that inspires loyalty and devotion, not just purchases.

CHAPTER 8: CRAFTING POWERFUL BRAND STORYTELLING AND CONNECTING THROUGH LANGUAGE AND EMOTION

In the world of branding, language is a powerful tool. It shapes perception, influences emotions, and drives action. How you communicate your brand story, your values, and your purpose will determine how deeply you resonate with your audience. One of the most effective ways to establish this connection is through **brand storytelling**—the art of using narratives to convey your brand's mission, values, and journey. Language, when used intentionally, becomes the bridge between your brand and your audience, allowing them to see, feel, and believe in your purpose.

This chapter focuses on how you can harness the power of **language and storytelling** to build a brand that truly connects with your audience. By telling stories that go beyond the features of your products and tap into emotions, shared values, and real-life experiences, you can create a brand that feels authentic and trustworthy. We'll explore how to craft a compelling brand story, the importance of sharing your "why," and how to use customer success stories as proof points for your brand's impact. We'll also delve into the value of authenticity and vulnerability in storytelling, making your brand more relatable in today's world.

The Role of Language in Brand Storytelling

Language is more than just words; it's a way of expressing who your brand is and what it stands for. The language you use in your storytelling helps shape how people perceive your brand and what emotions they associate with it. Whether it's a catchy slogan, a heartfelt narrative, or a casual and relatable tone, your brand's voice creates a deeper connection with your audience.

Through storytelling, you can highlight your **brand ethos**, reinforce your values, and communicate the purpose behind your business. When your audience feels like they understand your brand on an emotional level, they are more likely to trust and engage with you, leading to long-term loyalty. In short, the language you choose determines whether your audience simply hears you or truly connects with you.

Author's Insight

Words are powerful because they evoke emotions. When you tell your brand's story in a way that makes your audience feel understood and valued, you're not just selling a product—you're creating a relationship.

Crafting a Powerful Brand Story

A brand story is more than a timeline of your company's history—it's the **narrative that conveys the heart and soul** of your business. Your brand story should focus on the journey you've taken to solve a problem, why you're passionate about your mission, and how your brand is making an impact. The goal is to make your audience feel something, whether it's excitement, inspiration, or trust.

Key Elements of a Powerful Brand Story:
1. **The Problem:** Every great brand story begins with a problem that needed to be solved. Clearly define the issue that your brand set out to tackle, whether it's an unmet customer need, a broken industry standard, or a societal challenge. This makes your story relatable because your audience has likely faced the same problem.

Example: Glossier began with founder Emily Weiss's frustration with the complexity of beauty products. She realized that beauty routines were too complicated and inaccessible for many people. Glossier's story centers on simplifying skincare and makeup, making beauty more approachable for everyday women.

2. **The Journey:** Once you've established the problem, share your brand's journey in solving it. This involves detailing the challenges, obstacles, and milestones that have shaped your business. Audiences love rooting for brands that have faced adversity and come out stronger. The journey humanizes your brand, making it feel like an underdog story or a hero's quest.

Example: Nike's story is deeply tied to perseverance and overcoming challenges. The brand's "Just Do It" slogan is a nod to the journey of every athlete—facing obstacles, pushing through failures, and ultimately achieving greatness.

3. **The Transformation:** A great story shows growth and transformation. Highlight how your brand evolved from its humble beginnings to where it is today. Share how you've helped your customers or changed the industry. This part of the story is where you showcase the impact of your brand's journey.

Example: Peloton transformed the fitness industry by offering a connected home workout experience. Their brand story showcases how they've made fitness accessible, convenient, and community-driven for millions of people worldwide.

4. **The Values:** A brand story should always reflect your **core values**. Whether it's sustainability, innovation, inclusivity, or community, these values should be woven into your narrative. It helps customers understand not just what you do, but why you do it.

Example: Patagonia's brand story is deeply rooted in environmental activism. From their founding, they have maintained a commitment to sustainability, and their storytelling reflects their mission to protect the planet.

Author's Insight

Your brand story is the heartbeat of your business. It's not just about the facts—it's about the feeling. A powerful brand story should inspire your audience to see your brand as more than a product, but as a partner in their journey.

Telling Your 'Why' – The Core of Brand Storytelling

At the heart of every great brand is a compelling **'why'**— the purpose that drives everything you do. It's the reason your business exists beyond making a profit. The brands that truly resonate with their audiences are those that communicate this deeper meaning, showing that they are motivated by something bigger than just selling products.

Your 'why' is the key to differentiating your brand in a crowded market, inspiring loyalty, and connecting with customers on a personal level. When you tell your 'why,' you're sharing the passion, purpose, and values that fuel your brand. You're not just explaining what you do or how you do it—you're showing **why it matters**. This section will explore how to determine the **genesis** of your brand story and uncover the **universal drivers** that form the core of your mission.

Determining the Genesis of Your Story

Every brand has a starting point, a moment or experience that sparked the desire to create something meaningful. This origin story—your brand's genesis—is the foundation of your 'why.' It's essential to dig deep into your beginnings to identify the root cause of your business's existence. The more personal and authentic this story is, the more relatable it will be to your audience.

Your genesis is not just the **what** or **how** of your brand's inception, but the **why**—the emotional and universal drivers that led you to create your business. This origin story is what makes your brand unique, as it's rooted in your specific experiences, challenges, and vision for the future.

Steps to Uncover the Genesis of Your Brand Story:
1. **Reflect on Your Early Inspirations:**
   Go back to the very beginning—what inspired you to start your business? Was there a personal experience that triggered your desire to solve a problem? Were there specific events or moments in your life that made you realize the need for your product or service? This reflection is crucial in understanding the emotional foundation of your brand.

Example: Warby Parker's genesis began when one of its founders lost his glasses and was shocked by the high cost of replacing them. This frustration led to the realization that affordable, stylish eyewear was not widely accessible. Warby Parker's 'why' is rooted in a desire to disrupt the eyewear industry and make glasses more affordable and fashionable for everyone.

2. **Identify the Problem You Set Out to Solve:**
   Your brand's genesis is closely tied to the problem you set out to solve. What gap in the market did you notice? What issue were people facing that motivated you to create a solution? The bigger and more relatable the problem, the more compelling your story will be.

Example: Airbnb was born when its founders were struggling to pay rent in San Francisco. They saw an opportunity to offer affordable, short-term housing to travelers by renting out their own space. This problem—making housing more accessible and affordable—became the core of Airbnb's 'why.'

3. **Determine Your Universal Drivers:**
   While your brand story is personal, it must also tap into **universal drivers**—those deep, human needs and desires that resonate with everyone. Universal drivers include things like the need for connection, belonging, security, or self-expression. By aligning your 'why' with these universal drivers, you ensure that your story is not only relatable but emotionally impactful.

Example: Nike's universal driver is the pursuit of greatness. Their brand isn't just about selling shoes; it's about empowering people to push their limits and achieve their personal best. This emotional driver— the desire to overcome challenges and be extraordinary—is central to Nike's 'why.'

4. **Clarify Your Passion and Mission:**
   Your 'why' is also fueled by the **passion** that drives your business forward. What excites you about your work? What change do you want to see in the world, and how does your business contribute to that change? This passion should be clear in your brand story and should align with the problem you're solving.

Example: Ben & Jerry's is passionate about social justice and environmental sustainability. Their 'why' goes beyond selling ice cream; they aim to use their business to promote causes they care about, such as climate action and LGBTQ+ rights. Their passion for activism is an integral part of their brand story, making it resonate deeply with socially conscious customers.

Uncovering Your Universal Drivers: The Key to Emotional Connection

To make your 'why' truly compelling, you need to link it to **universal drivers**—the fundamental human emotions and motivations that are present in everyone. These drivers are the core reasons people buy from brands, beyond logic or practicality. When you tap into these emotional drivers, you create a deeper, more meaningful connection with your audience.

Common Universal Drivers Include:

1. **Belonging:** People have an innate need to feel part of a group or community. Brands that tap into this sense of belonging create loyal followings by offering more than just a product—they offer membership in a community.

Example: Harley-Davidson has built a cult following by tapping into the universal driver of belonging. Harley owners don't just buy motorcycles; they become part of a lifestyle and community that shares values of freedom and rebellion. The sense of identity and connection that comes with being a Harley rider is what drives their customers' loyalty.

2. **Empowerment:** Many successful brands make their customers feel empowered to achieve something, whether it's personal growth, professional success, or improved health. Brands that focus on empowerment often inspire and motivate their customers to take action.

Example: Peloton taps into the universal driver of empowerment by making fitness accessible to everyone, regardless of location or schedule. Their storytelling emphasizes personal growth, perseverance, and achievement, encouraging users to push through challenges and feel empowered in their fitness journey.

3. **Self-Expression:** Consumers want to align themselves with brands that reflect their values, identity, and lifestyle. When a brand taps into self-expression, it allows customers to express who they are through the products or services they use.

Example: Apple is a master at positioning its products as tools for self-expression. From the iPhone to the MacBook, Apple's marketing emphasizes creativity and individuality, appealing to customers who see themselves as innovators and creators.

4. **Security:** People crave stability and reassurance, especially in uncertain times. Brands that promise security—whether financial, emotional, or physical—are often able to build strong, trusting relationships with their customers.

Example: Allstate's "You're in Good Hands" campaign plays on the universal need for security. The insurance company's messaging reassures customers that they will be protected in times of uncertainty, creating a sense of trust and peace of mind.

5. **Adventure and Discovery:** Some brands thrive by appealing to the human desire for adventure and exploration. These brands tell stories that evoke curiosity, excitement, and the thrill of discovering something new.

Example: Patagonia taps into the universal driver of adventure with its brand story. The company's storytelling emphasizes exploration, environmental conservation, and the thrill of outdoor adventure, attracting customers who share a love for nature and discovery.

How to Effectively Communicate Your 'Why'

Once you've uncovered the genesis of your story and aligned it with universal drivers, the next step is to communicate your 'why' effectively. Your 'why' needs to be integrated into everything you do, from your brand messaging and marketing to your customer interactions.

Tips for Communicating Your 'Why' as Storytelling:

1. **Be Personal and Relatable:** When sharing your 'why,' use personal anecdotes and stories to bring it to life. People connect with personal experiences more than abstract ideas, so make your 'why' feel real and relatable.

Example: Glossier founder Emily Weiss often shares personal stories about her frustrations with traditional beauty products, which inspired her to create a brand focused on simplicity and ease. This personal narrative makes Glossier's 'why' feel authentic and relatable to its target audience.

2. **Keep It Simple and Clear:** Your 'why' should be easy to understand and communicate. Avoid jargon or overly complicated explanations—focus on the core mission that drives your brand and why it matters to your audience.

Example: TOMS' "One for One" model is a simple and clear way to communicate their 'why.' For every pair of shoes purchased, a pair is donated to someone in need. This straightforward messaging resonates with customers who want to support a socially conscious brand.

3. **Make It Emotional:** Tap into the emotions behind your 'why.' Whether it's passion for change, frustration with the status quo, or a desire to make the world a better place, your 'why' should evoke an emotional response from your audience.

Example: Nike's "Just Do It" campaign taps into the universal emotion of perseverance and the pursuit of greatness. Their 'why' is about inspiring people to push beyond their limits and achieve their personal best, making the brand feel motivational and empowering.

4. **Show, Don't Just Tell:** Back up your 'why' with actions. Show how your brand's mission is reflected in your business practices, products, and interactions with customers. Authenticity is key— customers can sense when a brand's 'why' is genuine or just a marketing ploy.

Example: Patagonia doesn't just talk about environmental activism—they show it through their actions. From their "Don't Buy This Jacket" campaign, which encouraged customers to repair their gear instead of buying new, to their commitment to using recycled materials, Patagonia consistently aligns their actions with their 'why.'

Using Your 'Why' to Build a Brand That Lasts

Your 'why' is the driving force behind your brand's story, mission, and success. By determining the genesis of your story and aligning it with universal drivers, you can create a powerful and emotional connection with your audience. Sharing your 'why' allows customers to see your brand as more than just a product—it becomes a movement, a reflection of their values, and a part of their identity.

Author's Insight

Your 'why' is what sets you apart in a world full of brands competing for attention. It's the emotional heartbeat of your business, the reason people will choose you and stay loyal to you. When you communicate your 'why' with passion and clarity, you're not just building a business— you're building a legacy.

Showcasing Customer Success Stories – Proof That Your Brand Delivers

While telling your brand's story and sharing your 'why' are powerful tools, nothing builds trust like **proof**. Customer success stories, case studies, and testimonials provide the evidence your audience needs to believe in your brand. These real-life stories show that your brand doesn't just talk the talk—it delivers results.

How to Use Customer Success Stories in Your Brand Storytelling:

- √ **Select the Right Stories:** Choose stories that showcase the transformation your product or service has made in the lives of your customers. Focus on stories that highlight the problems your brand has solved, and the positive outcomes achieved.

√ **Include Real Testimonials:** Let your customers speak for themselves. Use their words and experiences to demonstrate the value of your brand. Direct quotes and testimonials from satisfied customers add authenticity to your storytelling.

√ **Showcase Before-and-After Results:** Highlight the change your product or service has brought about in a tangible way. Before-and-after comparisons are a powerful way to illustrate the impact your brand has on real people.

√ **Humanize the Experience:** Don't just focus on the numbers or results—show the human side of the story. Share the emotional journey your customers went through and how your brand made their lives better.

This is Branding Example: Slack

Slack uses customer success stories to showcase how their platform has transformed the way teams communicate and collaborate. By sharing real-life case studies from companies that have benefited from using Slack, they demonstrate the impact their product has on efficiency and productivity. These stories humanize Slack's brand by showing the people behind the results.

Author's Insight

People trust people, not brands. Let your customers tell your story—it's more powerful than any marketing campaign.

Every brand has a story to tell—a narrative that encapsulates its essence, values, and the journey that defines it. Coupled with a distinct brand voice, this story can profoundly impact how your audience perceives and engages with your brand.

Your brand story is the pulse that turns your customers into believers and your business into a movement.

thisisbrandingbook.com

The Power of Authenticity and Vulnerability

In an age where consumers are constantly bombarded by curated, polished, and sometimes overly idealized content, **authenticity** and **vulnerability** have become two of the most powerful tools in brand storytelling. Gone are the days when customers were satisfied with a sleek advertisement that made a product look flawless.

Today, they crave real stories, transparency, and brands that reflect the genuine, human experience. When brands embrace authenticity and vulnerability, they foster deeper emotional connections with their audience, build trust, and ultimately create a more loyal customer base.

Being authentic means presenting your brand as it truly is—its strengths, values, and even its flaws. Vulnerability, on the other hand, goes one step further by allowing you to share the challenges, failures, and struggles that come with building a brand.

By exposing these aspects of your journey, you show your audience that you are not just a business, but a collective of real people working through real issues. This level of openness resonates in a world where so much of what we see online is filtered and curated.

In this chapter, we'll explore why authenticity and vulnerability are key in brand storytelling and how they can help you build stronger relationships with your customers.

Why Authenticity and Vulnerability Matter

Authenticity and vulnerability are not just buzzwords— they are central to creating trust and emotional engagement. In fact, research shows that **91% of consumers are willing to reward a brand for its authenticity through purchases, loyalty, and sharing**. People want to feel like they're buying from a brand they can relate to and trust, not just another faceless corporation.

Here's why these elements are so essential in brand storytelling:

1. They Build Trust: Trust is the foundation of any meaningful relationship, and this is especially true in the relationship between a brand and its customers. By being transparent and genuine, your brand becomes more trustworthy. When consumers see that you're not trying to hide behind corporate jargon or an overly polished facade, they feel more confident in your brand's intentions and promises. Sharing your struggles and failures—those moments when things didn't go as planned—humanizes your brand. It shows that you're not perfect, just like your customers, and that you're constantly learning and evolving. This humility makes your audience feel more connected to your brand because they see you as real.

2. They Create Emotional Connections: Emotions drive purchasing decisions far more than logic does. Brands that can tap into their audience's emotions are the ones that win their hearts and their loyalty. Authenticity and vulnerability allow you to tell stories that are **relatable**, **inspiring**, and often **touching**. They allow you to go beyond selling products and instead create experiences that resonate deeply with your customers. For instance, sharing the story of how your brand struggled to get off the ground but persisted through adversity can inspire others who are facing similar challenges. It can make your audience root for you and want to support you—not just because they like your product, but because they believe in your journey.

3. They Differentiate Your Brand: In today's crowded market, standing out can be a challenge. Brands that embrace authenticity and vulnerability differentiate themselves by showing that they're not just in it for the profit—they have a mission, a story, and a set of values that guide them. When you tell your story authentically, you show what makes your brand different from competitors who may offer similar products or services but lack a strong emotional connection with their audience. Being vulnerable also shows that you're willing to take risks.

While some brands play it safe by only sharing successes, those that are open about their failures are seen as braver and more transparent. This sets you apart in a marketplace where consumers are increasingly skeptical of overly curated content and marketing that feels "too good to be true."

How to Use Authenticity and Vulnerability in Brand Storytelling

To effectively leverage authenticity and vulnerability in your storytelling, you need to go beyond surface-level transparency. It's not enough to just say that you care about your customers or that your brand is "real"—you need to **show it**. Here are actionable ways to incorporate these elements into your brand's story:

1. Share Your Challenges and Failures

Every business has faced challenges, whether it's a failed product launch, a tough financial year, or a major setback in the early stages. Instead of hiding these struggles, embrace them as part of your story. Sharing these vulnerable moments not only humanizes your brand but also shows that you have the resilience to overcome adversity.

Example: Everlane, the ethical fashion brand, is known for its transparency in every aspect of its business, from pricing to sourcing materials. However, what truly sets them apart is how they handle their mistakes. When they failed to meet sustainability goals or faced delays in product development, Everlane openly communicated these challenges to their customers, explaining what went wrong and how they were working to fix it. This level of vulnerability has earned them the trust and loyalty of customers who appreciate their honesty.

2. Use a Personal, Relatable Voice

Authenticity shines through in how you communicate. Your brand's voice should feel natural and reflective of your values. Avoid overly corporate or robotic language, and instead, speak to your audience as you would to a friend. Whether your tone is playful, serious, inspirational, or down-to-earth, make sure it feels **authentic to your brand**.

Use real stories and personal anecdotes to make your brand more relatable. If you started your business in your garage, share that detail. If your product was inspired by a personal experience or frustration, let your audience know. People connect with **stories**, not sales pitches.

Example: Glossier, the beauty brand, has mastered the art of using a relatable, conversational tone in its storytelling. Their founder, Emily Weiss, often shares her personal experiences and frustrations with the beauty industry, making the brand feel approachable and authentic. Glossier's tone on social media and in marketing campaigns feels like a conversation with a friend, which has helped build a loyal community of customers who feel personally connected to the brand.

3. Be Transparent About Your Values and Actions
Consumers today are more concerned about what a brand stands for than ever before. They want to know that the companies they support are aligned with their own values, whether that's sustainability, social justice, inclusivity, or ethical practices. Being transparent about your brand's values, and showing how you live up to them, is a critical part of building trust. If you're committed to sustainability, for example, be open about the steps you're taking—even if you're not perfect. Let your customers know where you're succeeding and where you're still working to improve. Transparency builds credibility, especially when you admit that you're not perfect but are striving to be better.

Example: Patagonia has built its brand on environmental activism, but what sets them apart is their transparency. They regularly share the environmental impact of their products, and when they can't achieve 100% sustainability, they are upfront about the challenges they face. This level of transparency has earned Patagonia immense respect and loyalty from consumers who appreciate the brand's honesty and commitment to its values.

4. Engage in Meaningful Conversations with Your Audience
Authenticity isn't just about the stories you tell—it's also about how you interact with your audience. Show that you're listening by engaging in **real conversations** with your customers. Respond to their comments on social

media, address their concerns, and ask for their feedback. Customers who feel heard are more likely to develop a deep emotional connection to your brand. This interaction should be **two-way**. Don't just post content and expect your audience to engage. Ask them questions, solicit their opinions, and make them feel like they are part of your brand's journey. Being vulnerable means being open to feedback, both positive and negative.

Example: Lush, the handmade cosmetics brand, is known for its open dialogue with customers. They actively engage with their audience on social media, respond to comments and concerns, and even take product suggestions from their community. Lush also doesn't shy away from admitting when something goes wrong, such as product recalls or environmental impact concerns, fostering trust and loyalty through honest communication.

The Benefits of Authentic and Vulnerable Storytelling
When you embrace authenticity and vulnerability, your brand reaps several benefits that go beyond short-term gains. These storytelling techniques help you build a **cult-like following** of customers who are emotionally invested in your brand, rather than simply transactional buyers.

1. Increased Customer Loyalty
Brands that are authentic and transparent build lasting relationships with their customers. When people feel like they know the real story behind your brand and trust your values, they are more likely to remain loyal to your products or services over time. Loyalty extends beyond repeat purchases—your customers will advocate for your brand, recommend it to others, and defend it when needed.

2. Emotional Engagement

Vulnerable and authentic storytelling taps into emotions like empathy, inspiration, and trust. When your audience feels something in response to your story, they are more likely to form a **deeper emotional connection** with your brand. Emotional engagement is a key driver of long-term brand success because it's not easily replaced by competitors.

3. Greater Credibility

Being vulnerable and open about your brand's journey, including the challenges and failures, increases your **credibility**. Customers are more likely to believe in your brand when they see that you are not hiding behind a perfect image. Instead of pretending to be flawless, your brand shows that it's real, which builds trust.

4. Differentiation from Competitors

In a saturated market, authenticity is a key differentiator. Brands that are willing to be open and vulnerable stand out because they feel more human. Instead of trying to blend in with polished, glossy advertising, your brand becomes **distinct** because it embraces imperfections, shares real stories, and connects on a personal level.

The Power of Real Connection

Authenticity and vulnerability are no longer optional—they are essential elements of brand storytelling in today's world. Consumers want to support brands that reflect their own values and experiences, brands that are willing to show their human side and be real. By sharing your struggles, using a personal voice, being transparent about your values, and engaging with your audience, you can create a brand that stands out, builds trust, and fosters deep emotional connections.

Brand storytelling isn't just about promoting your products—it's about creating a narrative that connects with your audience on a deeper level. By sharing your 'why,' showcasing customer success stories, and being authentic in your messaging, you can build a brand that people don't just buy from—they believe in. When your brand becomes part of your audience's story, you've succeeded in creating a lasting, meaningful connection.

Author's Insight

The most powerful stories aren't the ones that are perfect—they're the ones that are real. When your brand shows authenticity and vulnerability, you invite your audience into your story, making them part of your journey. And that's what creates lasting loyalty.

> Good stories surprise us. They make us think and feel. They stick in our minds and help us remember ideas and concepts in a way that a PowerPoint crammed with bar graphs never can.

Shane Snow, The Storytelling Edge

WORKSHEET: CRAFTING YOUR STORY

Brand values are the guiding principles that define who you are and what you stand for. By defining your values, identifying your story, and connecting it with your audience you build the foundation for a compelling brand story that resonates and inspires.

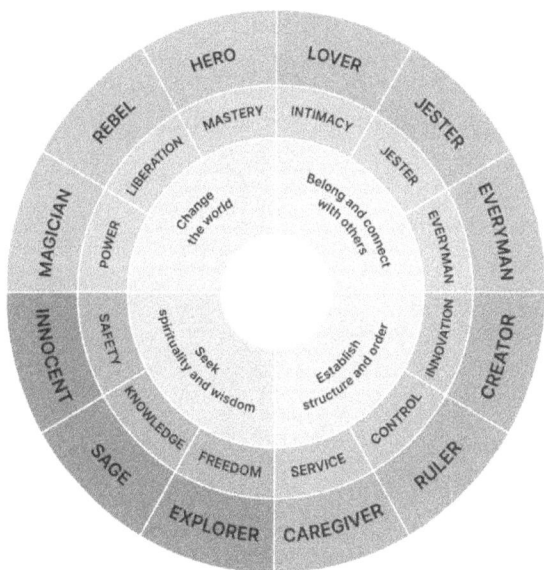

Fig. 2: Brand Archetypes Framework

What inspired you to start your business, and what problem were you passionate about solving?"

This question taps into the heart of your brand's origin and purpose, laying the foundation for a meaningful and authentic brand story.

What pivotal moment or experience in your journey led you to create your brand, and how does this connect with the problem your audience faces today?"

Tip: Think about a challenge or personal realization that inspired you to start your business.

Write Your Answer:

FOUNDATION OF YOUR STORY:

- Reflect on your brand's mission and vision statements. Consider the journey of your brand from its inception to the present.

- Identify key milestones, challenges overcome, and the overarching mission that propelled your brand forward.

CHARACTERS AND PLOT:

- Define the main characters in your story. Typically, this includes the founders, employees, and customers.

- Describe the plot by outlining how your brand has made a difference in the lives of its customers or community.

EMOTIONAL CONNECTION:

- Pinpoint the emotions you want your story to evoke in the audience. Should they feel inspired, comforted, excited?

- We have these emotions into the fabric of your narrative to ensure it resonates deeply with your audience.

DRAFTING YOUR STORY:

- Combine the elements above into a cohesive narrative. Start with the background, introduce the characters, describe the journey, highlight the struggles, and celebrate the victories.

These structures can be used to craft compelling narratives that resonate with your audience by helping guide your brand storytelling efforts.

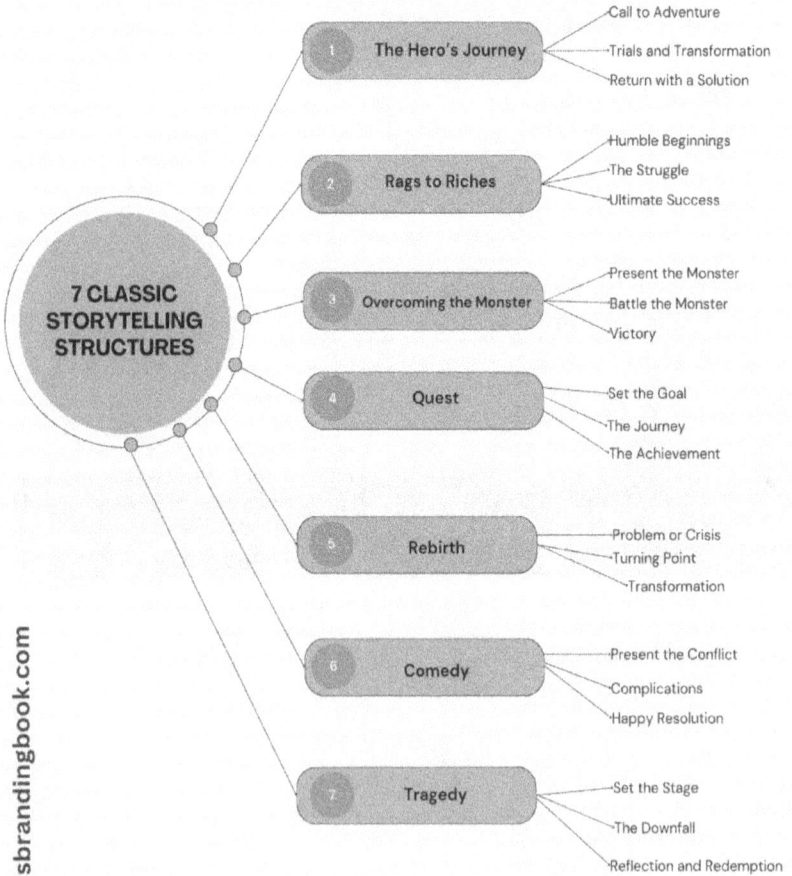

7 CLASSIC STORYTELLING STRUCTURES

1. **The Hero's Journey**
   - Call to Adventure
   - Trials and Transformation
   - Return with a Solution

2. **Rags to Riches**
   - Humble Beginnings
   - The Struggle
   - Ultimate Success

3. **Overcoming the Monster**
   - Present the Monster
   - Battle the Monster
   - Victory

4. **Quest**
   - Set the Goal
   - The Journey
   - The Achievement

5. **Rebirth**
   - Problem or Crisis
   - Turning Point
   - Transformation

6. **Comedy**
   - Present the Conflict
   - Complications
   - Happy Resolution

7. **Tragedy**
   - Set the Stage
   - The Downfall
   - Reflection and Redemption

thisisbrandingbook.com

CHAPTER 9:
BECOMING THE VISIONARY—THE
DEVELOPMENT OF YOUR PERSONAL BRAND

Personal branding is the art of shaping how others perceive you, aligning your unique skills, personality, and experiences to create a distinct and compelling identity. In today's digital landscape, **being the leader of your personal brand** is essential for driving recognition, awareness, and long-term success. Whether you're an entrepreneur, small business owner, or professional, building a strong personal brand not only enhances your career but also amplifies the value of your business.

Personal branding goes beyond self-promotion—it's about defining a **consistent narrative** that reflects your core values, expertise, and the **impact** you want to make. As the visionary of your brand, you must position yourself as an authority, inspire others through your story, and leverage your influence to create opportunities. By establishing yourself as the face of your personal brand, you set the stage for long-term success and recognition.

In this chapter, we'll explore the importance of personal branding, how to lead with authenticity, maintain visibility, build consistency, and stand out in today's crowded marketplace. We'll also dive into real-world examples of how personal brands can drive business success, highlighting key strategies for becoming a leader in your field.

The Power of Personal Branding for Entrepreneurs

In today's digital age, where visibility and authenticity are critical to success, **personal branding** has become a strategic asset for entrepreneurs. Unlike a corporate brand, which focuses on a company's image, personal branding is about defining and promoting **who you are** as an individual. It's the process of creating a distinct identity that reflects your unique talents, values, expertise, and the experiences that set you apart. As an entrepreneur, your personal brand becomes a powerful tool that not only elevates your professional credibility but also drives the success of your business.

Personal branding is no longer a luxury—it's a necessity. It gives you the ability to control how people perceive you, and it shapes the narrative of your professional journey. Entrepreneurs who invest in building their personal brands are better positioned to attract opportunities, build trust with their audience, and enhance their business brand's visibility.

Why Personal Branding Matters for Entrepreneurs

The modern consumer wants more than just a transaction—they seek a connection. They are increasingly interested in the people behind the brands they support. This shift in consumer behavior has made personal branding essential for entrepreneurs who want to stand out in crowded markets and create lasting relationships with customers, clients, and partners.

When you build a strong personal brand, you become the **face of your business**, representing its values, mission, and purpose. People are more likely to trust a business when they feel connected to the person leading it. Personal branding allows you to humanize your company, making it more approachable and relatable.

Here are some key reasons why personal branding is so important for entrepreneurs:

1. Building Trust and Credibility
Trust is the foundation of any successful business relationship. A well-established personal brand fosters **authenticity** and **credibility**. When people know who you are, what you stand for, and what value you bring, they are more likely to trust you—and by extension, trust your business.

By showcasing your expertise, sharing your personal journey, and consistently delivering value through your brand's messaging, you build a reputation as an authority in your industry. This credibility opens doors to new opportunities, whether it's attracting investors, clients, or business partners.

2. Attracting New Opportunities
A strong personal brand acts as a **magnet** for opportunities. Entrepreneurs with a well-defined brand are more likely to attract media coverage, speaking engagements, and networking prospects. Personal branding helps you stand out in competitive spaces, making it easier for others to recognize your value.

When you lead with your personal brand, potential clients or collaborators feel like they know you before they even meet you. This familiarity breaks down barriers and creates a sense of trust that can lead to new business deals, partnerships, or career advancement.

3. Enhancing Your Business Brand

For entrepreneurs, personal branding and business branding often go hand in hand. Your personal reputation directly impacts how your company is perceived. Entrepreneurs like **Elon Musk** and **Sara Blakely** have built powerful personal brands that amplify the visibility and trustworthiness of their respective businesses—Tesla, SpaceX, and Spanx. Their personal success stories, public appearances, and social media presence help shape how their businesses are viewed.

Your personal brand can be a significant asset to your business, as customers often associate the values and character of a company with the individual leading it. This connection can make your business more relatable, engaging, and trustworthy in the eyes of your target audience.

4. Building a Loyal Following

One of the greatest benefits of personal branding is the ability to build a **loyal community** of followers who believe in your mission and vision. When people connect with you on a personal level, they become more than customers—they become advocates for your brand. This community of supporters can amplify your message, share your content, and provide valuable word-of-mouth marketing.

As you continue to engage with your audience through social media, blogs, podcasts, and public speaking, you deepen the connection and foster long-term loyalty. A loyal following not only generates consistent revenue but also provides feedback, ideas, and support to help your business grow.

The Role of Personal Branding in the Digital Age
Today, where everyone has a platform, personal branding has taken on a new level of importance. Social media, online publications, podcasts, and other digital platforms provide entrepreneurs with unprecedented opportunities to **share their stories** and **showcase their expertise**. With a few clicks, you can reach thousands—or even millions—of people.

However, with this accessibility comes the challenge of standing out. In a world where personal brands are constantly vying for attention, authenticity, and consistency become even more crucial. Personal branding is not just about self-promotion; it's about delivering consistent value to your audience and staying true to your core values.

Platforms like LinkedIn, Instagram, and Twitter have become essential tools for personal branding. They allow entrepreneurs to communicate their ideas, interact with followers, and share their expertise on a global scale. By regularly producing high-quality content and engaging with your audience, you can establish yourself as a thought leader in your field.

This is Branding Example: Marie Forleo
One of the best examples of an entrepreneur who has built a powerful personal brand is **Marie Forleo**, founder of

MarieTV and the B-School online business program. Forleo has crafted a personal brand around the idea of empowering individuals—especially women—to build businesses and create the lives they want. Her personal brand is infused with energy, positivity, and a strong commitment to helping others succeed.

Through consistent content creation, including weekly videos, motivational posts, and courses, Forleo has amassed a loyal following of entrepreneurs and creatives who view her as a mentor. Her personal brand has not only elevated her own career but has also made B-School one of the most recognized online business programs in the world.

Forleo's success demonstrates how a personal brand built on authenticity, expertise, and consistent engagement can drive business growth and recognition.

Author's Insight

Personal branding is not just a tool—it's the heart of your entrepreneurial journey. When you lead with authenticity and share your true self with the world, you create a connection that goes beyond business transactions. You build trust, loyalty, and a legacy that resonates with your audience.

For entrepreneurs, personal branding is more than just a way to market yourself—it's a pathway to influence, recognition, and business success. By building trust, attracting new opportunities, enhancing your business brand, and cultivating a loyal following, you establish yourself as a leader in your industry.

In today's fast-paced, digital-first world, the entrepreneurs who stand out are those who invest in developing their personal brands. By leading with authenticity, staying visible, and consistently providing value to your audience, you can create a personal brand that drives lasting success.

Remember, your personal brand is the story that people will talk about you when you're not in the room. Make sure it's a story worth sharing.

Leading with Authenticity: The Key to Personal Branding
At the core of every powerful personal brand is **authenticity**. Being authentic means staying true to who you are, reflecting your genuine values and beliefs in every action and communication. In a world filled with perfectly curated content, authenticity is what cuts through the noise and builds genuine connections.

Why Authenticity Matters
In today's marketplace, people crave transparency. They want to connect with real individuals, not facades or overly polished personas. Authenticity fosters **trust** and **loyalty**, making your brand relatable and human. When you lead with authenticity, you create deeper relationships with your audience because they feel they know the real you.

The Benefits of Being Authentic:
- √ **Build Stronger Relationships:** Authenticity allows you to connect on a personal level. When people feel they can trust you, they're more likely to engage with your content, buy your products, or seek your services.

- √ **Increased Engagement:** Authentic content—whether it's blog posts, videos, or social media updates—tends to perform better because it resonates more with audiences looking for realness in a sea of superficiality.
- √ **Sustainable Growth:** Authentic brands don't just gain followers—they build loyal communities. People stay connected to brands they believe are honest and transparent.

This is Branding Example: Gary Vaynerchuk

Gary Vaynerchuk, a well-known entrepreneur and marketing expert, is a prime example of authenticity in personal branding. Known for his no-nonsense, honest, and sometimes brash style, Gary Vee consistently shares both his successes and his failures, making his audience feel like they're part of his journey. His authenticity has helped him build a massive following across platforms and cement his place as an influential thought leader in marketing and entrepreneurship.

Author's Insight

Authenticity is the foundation of trust. When you show people who you really are, they'll connect with you on a deeper level and become loyal advocates for your brand.

Visibility: Getting Your Personal Brand Noticed

Even the most authentic personal brand won't have much impact if it's invisible. **Visibility** is about showing up consistently in the right places, whether that's on social media, at industry events, or through public speaking. The more visible you are, the more opportunities you create to engage with your audience and grow your brand.

The Importance of Visibility
Visibility ensures that people see and interact with your personal brand regularly. It's not just about being active on social media, but about being **strategic** in where and how you show up. Whether through blog posts, videos, interviews, or public speaking, your visibility reinforces your authority and keeps your brand top of mind.

How to Increase Your Visibility:
√ **Be Active on Social Media:** Social platforms like X [formerly Twitter], LinkedIn, and Instagram are powerful tools for building your personal brand. Share content regularly, engage with your audience, and join relevant conversations in your industry.

√ **Attend Industry Events:** Speaking at conferences or networking events helps you get in front of key decision-makers and potential clients. Even attending as a guest allows you to build relationships and enhance your brand's visibility.

√ **Leverage Media Coverage:** Seek opportunities to contribute to blogs, podcasts, or news outlets as an expert in your field. Media exposure helps position you as a leader and broadens your reach to new audiences.

This is Branding Example: Brene Brown
Brene Brown, a researcher and author known for her work on vulnerability and shame, became a global sensation after her TED Talk went viral. By consistently sharing her insights across multiple platforms—books, social media, podcasts, and speaking events—she built a personal brand centered around authenticity and emotional intelligence. Her visibility and consistent messaging

helped her become a household name in personal development.

Author's Insight
Visibility is key to success. It's not enough to be great at what you do—you need to make sure people know about it. Show up consistently and let the world see your value.

Building Consistency in Your Personal Brand

Consistency is the secret ingredient that transforms a good personal brand into a memorable one. It ensures that your messaging, tone, visuals, and values remain aligned across every platform and interaction. Whether someone encounters your LinkedIn profile, watches a YouTube video, or attends one of your presentations, they should experience a **consistent brand**.

Consistency Matters

Consistency builds **trust** and **recognition**. When you show up consistently with the same tone, message, and style, people begin to associate your brand with a particular experience or expertise. Inconsistent messaging, on the other hand, can confuse your audience and dilute your brand's impact.

The Benefits of Consistency:

- √ **Stronger Recognition:** Consistent branding helps people remember who you are and what you stand for. It makes your brand recognizable in a crowded marketplace.
- √ **Professionalism:** When your personal brand is consistent, it communicates professionalism. It shows that you take your brand seriously and are intentional about how you present yourself.

√ **Increased Trust:** Audiences are more likely to trust a brand that consistently delivers on its promises. Consistency reassures people that they can rely on you for valuable insights, services, or products.

How to Maintain Consistency in Personal Branding:
√ **Develop a Brand Style Guide:** Create guidelines for your tone of voice, color scheme, fonts, and messaging to ensure that all your content aligns with your personal brand identity.
√ **Use Scheduling Tools:** Platforms like Buffer or Hootsuite can help you plan and schedule content in advance, making it easier to stay consistent in your messaging and presence across different channels.
√ **Monitor Your Brand's Touchpoints:** Regularly check your website, social media, and public profiles to ensure that your messaging and visuals are consistent.

This is Branding Example: Oprah Winfrey
Oprah Winfrey is one of the most consistent personal brands in the world. Whether through her talk show, OWN network, or public speaking engagements, Oprah's brand consistently reflects her values of empowerment, education, and personal growth. Her messaging and tone remain authentic and aligned with her mission, making her one of the most trusted figures in media.

Author's Insight
Consistency is what turns followers into fans. When your audience knows what to expect from you, they're more likely to trust and stick with your brand over time.

How to Stand Out with Your Personal Brand

In today's hyper-competitive digital landscape, standing out is more important than ever. With so many professionals, entrepreneurs, and influencers vying for attention, your personal brand needs to be distinct, memorable, and aligned with your audience's needs.

What Makes a Personal Brand Stand Out?

√ **Niche Expertise:** Define a specific area of expertise where you can add unique value. The more focused your niche, the easier it is to stand out as a go-to expert in that field.

√ **Unique Perspective:** Your personal brand should reflect your distinct point of view, values, and experiences. What makes your story different from others in your industry? What insights can you offer that no one else can?

√ **Quality Content:** Creating valuable content is essential for standing out. Whether it's blog posts, podcasts, videos, or social media updates, focus on providing content that solves problems, educates, or entertains your audience.

This is Branding Example: Simon Sinek

Simon Sinek, author of **Start with Why**, built his personal brand around the simple but powerful concept of purpose-driven leadership. By consistently sharing insights about leadership and motivation through his books, TED Talks, and social media, Sinek has become a leading voice in his field. His unique perspective on leadership and purpose has set him apart from other business authors and speakers.

Leading Your Personal Brand to Success

Building a strong personal brand is more than just a marketing strategy—it's about defining who you are, what you stand for, and how you want to impact the world. By being authentic, maintaining visibility, staying consistent, and standing out with your unique perspective, you can create a personal brand that drives recognition, awareness, and lasting success.

Author's Insight

Standing out isn't about being flashy—it's about being memorable for the right reasons. Define what makes you unique, focus on delivering value, and don't be afraid to share your story with the world. You are the leader of your brand. When you take control of your narrative, show up consistently, and connect with your audience on a deep, authentic level, you create a brand that not only stands out but leaves a lasting legacy.

PERSONAL BRANDING WORKSHEET: CRAFTING A STRONG PERSONAL BRAND

Use the following questions to define and develop your personal brand. These prompts will help you clarify your values, identity, and the message you want to convey to your audience.

1. Defining Your Unique Identity
- √ What are the key strengths and skills that set you apart from others in your field?
- √ How do you want people to describe you when they first meet or hear about you?
- √ What personal experiences have shaped your professional journey?

2. Clarifying Your Values
- √ What are the core values you live by, and how do they influence your work?
- √ Which causes or beliefs are you most passionate about that align with your personal and professional life?
- √ How can you incorporate these values into your brand message?

3. Identifying Your Target Audience
- √ Who do you want to connect with, serve, or influence through your personal brand?
- √ What are the biggest challenges or pain points of your target audience?
- √ How can your expertise solve their problems or enhance their lives?

4. Crafting Your Personal Brand Message
√ What is your personal brand's mission or purpose?
√ How does your story or journey connect to your audience's needs and aspirations?
√ In one sentence, how would you summarize the core message of your personal brand?

5. Building Consistency Across Platforms
√ What tone and voice best represent your personality? Is it formal, casual, or somewhere in between?
√ How can you ensure that your visual identity (colors, fonts, imagery) is consistent across social media, your website, and other platforms?
√ What key messages or phrases will you use regularly to maintain consistency?

6. Enhancing Visibility and Engagement
√ Which platforms or channels will you use to showcase your personal brand?
√ How will you engage with your audience and build relationships through content, comments, or direct interaction?
√ What are 2-3 topics or themes you can consistently create content around to showcase your expertise?

7. Showcasing Authenticity and Vulnerability
√ What personal challenges or obstacles have you overcome that can inspire or connect with your audience?
√ How can you share your authentic self—both strengths and struggles—without compromising your professionalism?

CHAPTER 10:
LEVERAGING AI TO ENHANCE YOUR BRANDING

Artificial Intelligence (AI) has rapidly evolved from being a futuristic concept to an integral part of everyday business. From streamlining processes to improving customer experiences, AI is reshaping industries and offering brands new ways to grow, engage, and connect with their audience. As AI continues to advance, its role in branding is becoming more significant. Brands that harness the power of AI can enhance personalization, better understand customer emotions, and engage their audience more effectively—all of which builds brand loyalty and increases long-term value.

In this chapter, we'll explore how AI can transform your branding strategy. We'll look at how AI-driven personalization creates deeper customer connections, how sentiment analysis can give you insights into customer perception, and how AI-powered tools can improve customer service and engagement. By leveraging AI effectively, your brand can stay ahead of the competition and build a stronger, more connected relationship with your audience.

The Rise of AI and Its Impact on Branding

AI is no longer just a buzzword; it's a powerful tool that's transforming the way businesses operate. From automated customer service to predictive analytics, AI is reshaping the landscape of business, marketing, and branding. One of the most significant ways AI impacts branding is by allowing companies to create hyper-personalized experiences at scale. Brands can now use AI to analyze massive amounts of data and deliver targeted content, offers, and experiences that resonate with individual customers.

The rise of AI is a game-changer for brands because it allows for:

- √ **Efficiency**: AI automates time-consuming tasks like data analysis, content creation, and customer support, freeing up teams to focus on strategy and creativity.
- √ **Scalability**: AI enables brands to offer personalized experiences to thousands or even millions of customers simultaneously, something that would be impossible with traditional methods.
- √ **Precision**: AI can analyze customer data in real-time, helping brands deliver the right message to the right person at the right time.

AI Builds Brand Currency

Brand currency refers to the perceived value of your brand in the eyes of your customers. It's built through trust, relevance, and meaningful connections. AI plays a critical role in increasing brand currency by enhancing the customer experience and delivering value in new and innovative ways. When customers feel that your brand understands them, meets their needs, and provides personalized solutions, your brand's value increases.

Here are a few ways AI can build your brand currency:
- √ **Deeper Personalization**: AI allows brands to go beyond demographics and target customers based on behavior, preferences, and emotions, delivering content and products that are truly relevant to their individual needs.
- √ **Real-Time Engagement**: AI-driven chatbots and automated customer service ensure that customers receive timely support, creating a positive experience that reinforces trust in the brand.
- √ **Data-Driven Insights**: AI tools analyze customer data to predict future behaviors, helping brands stay one step ahead by anticipating customer needs and offering proactive solutions.

AI, when used correctly, can elevate a brand's relationship with its audience, creating lasting loyalty and increasing brand currency.

AI-Drives Personalization for Deeper Connections
AI-driven personalization is the use of machine learning algorithms to tailor experiences, content, and product recommendations to individual customers based on their behaviors, preferences, and interactions with your brand. Unlike traditional segmentation (which might target large groups of people based on age or location), AI-driven

personalization creates individualized experiences that feel uniquely tailored to each customer.

Personalization Matters for Branding

In today's market, customers expect personalization. They're used to the likes of Amazon and Netflix, which serve up tailored recommendations based on past behavior. Personalization makes customers feel valued and understood, which builds trust and strengthens brand loyalty. Brands that fail to offer personalized experiences risk losing customers to competitors who can.

AI analyzes data from various sources—such as customer purchase history, browsing behavior, and social media activity—to predict what individual customers are likely to want or need. It can then deliver personalized product recommendations, content, emails, and even website experiences that align with each customer's preferences.

Ways to Leverage AI-Driven Personalization

- √ **Personalized Product Recommendations**: Use AI algorithms to recommend products based on a customer's previous purchases, searches, or preferences. This not only improves the customer experience but also increases sales.
- √ **Dynamic Website Content**: AI can tailor the content on your website to match each visitor's preferences and behaviors. For instance, if a visitor frequently browses eco-friendly products, your homepage could display more sustainable options.
- √ **Targeted Email Campaigns**: AI can help you send personalized emails to customers based on their past interactions with your brand. Personalized emails that feature products or content relevant to

a customer's interests have higher open and conversion rates.

√ **Customized Ad Experiences**: AI can optimize your ad targeting by delivering personalized ads based on a user's online behavior and preferences, increasing the chances of engagement and conversion.

This is Branding Example: Spotify
Spotify's "Discover Weekly" playlist is a prime example of AI-driven personalization. Every Monday, Spotify delivers a curated playlist to each user, tailored to their music preferences based on past listening habits. This personalized experience not only keeps users engaged but also creates a deeper connection with the brand.

Author's Insight
Personalization is the future of branding. AI makes it possible to create one-to-one connections with customers, turning generic experiences into meaningful interactions.

Sentiment Analysis: Understanding How Customers Feel About Your Brand
Sentiment analysis is an AI-driven technique that analyzes written content (such as reviews, social media posts, and customer feedback) to determine the emotional tone behind the words. It helps brands understand how customers feel about their products, services, or overall brand—whether they're satisfied, frustrated, or excited.

Understanding customer sentiment is essential for building a brand that resonates with your audience.

Positive sentiment indicates that your brand is hitting the mark, while negative sentiment can signal areas for improvement. Sentiment analysis gives you real-time insights into customer perceptions, allowing you to respond quickly and adjust your strategy as needed.

Using Sentiment Analysis to Enhance Your Brand

√ **Monitor Brand Reputation**: AI tools can analyze mentions of your brand across social media, forums, and review sites to track overall sentiment. Are people talking positively about your brand, or are there common complaints that need to be addressed?

√ **Improve Customer Service**: Sentiment analysis can help you identify customers who are dissatisfied or frustrated based on the tone of their messages. You can then proactively reach out to these customers to resolve their issues and improve their experience.

√ **Optimize Marketing Campaigns**: By analyzing customer feedback on your marketing campaigns, you can determine which messages resonate the most and adjust your future content accordingly.

√ **Predict Customer Behavior**: Sentiment analysis can help predict future customer behavior. For example, consistently positive feedback from customers could indicate that they are likely to become repeat buyers or brand advocates.

This is Branding Example: Coca-Cola

Coca-Cola uses sentiment analysis to monitor social media conversations and measure customer sentiment in real-time. This allows the brand to track how customers feel about its products and marketing campaigns and adjust strategies based on the feedback.

Sentiment analysis is like having a window into your customers' minds. It helps you see not just what they're saying, but how they feel about your brand—and that's where the real insights lie.

AI Tools for Customer Service and Brand Engagement
We've all been there; we have an issue with a purchase we made and we want answers immediately. We want brands to be responsive to us and with urgency. Customers expect quick and efficient responses to their questions and issues. AI-powered customer service tools—such as chatbots and virtual assistants—allow brands to provide real-time support, 24/7. These tools improve the customer experience by answering questions instantly, resolving issues quickly, and reducing the burden on human customer service teams.

AI also enhances brand engagement by enabling brands to respond to customers in real-time, providing personalized recommendations and fostering stronger relationships.

Top AI Tools for Customer Service and Brand Engagement
AI-powered tools are transforming how businesses interact with their customers, making brand engagement more efficient and personalized. These tools not only help manage customer service but also strengthen your brand's connection with its audience. Below are some of the best AI tools to boost customer service and brand engagement:

1. ManyChat

ManyChat is an AI-driven chatbot platform that automates customer engagement on platforms like **Facebook Messenger, Instagram, WhatsApp**, and more. It helps brands connect with customers instantly, streamlining customer support, lead generation, and even sales.

Key Features:
- √ Automates customer support, lead nurturing, and feedback collection.
- √ Seamless integration with e-commerce platforms for real-time order status updates and product recommendations.
- √ Personalized messaging flows for a more interactive user experience.

Benefits for Brand Engagement:
- √ Enhances customer interactions with personalized, immediate responses.
- √ Builds stronger relationships by creating tailored customer experiences.
- √ Consistent engagement across multiple platforms reinforces brand loyalty.

2. Drift

Drift is a conversational marketing platform that uses AI-powered chatbots to create personalized customer experiences in real-time. It helps businesses convert website visitors into leads and enhance customer service.

Key Features:
- √ AI-powered chatbots for instant customer interactions and lead generation.
- √ Personalized conversations based on user behavior.
- √ Integration with CRM and marketing tools for seamless data flow.

Benefits for Brand Engagement:
- √ Increases customer interaction and lead conversion through real-time conversations.
- √ Consistent branding and messaging across customer touchpoints.
- √ Provides 24/7 support, increasing customer satisfaction.

3. Zendesk

Zendesk is a comprehensive customer service platform that uses AI to streamline ticketing systems and automate customer service. It helps businesses manage inquiries from various channels while maintaining consistent brand messaging.

Key Features:
- √ AI-powered chatbots for instant responses and ticket management.
- √ Cross-channel support (email, chat, phone, social media).
- √ Machine learning to prioritize and categorize support tickets.

Benefits for Brand Engagement:
- √ Ensures seamless customer experience across all touchpoints.
- √ AI learns from interactions to continuously improve service quality.
- √ Enhances customer satisfaction through quicker and more accurate responses.

4. Intercom

Intercom offers an AI-driven platform for customer engagement, using chatbots to handle customer queries, nurture leads, and enhance the customer experience. It enables real-time conversations and data-driven personalization.

Key Features:
- √ AI chatbots for lead qualification and customer support.
- √ Customizable conversation flows to align with brand tone.
- √ In-app messaging, web chat, and email for cross-channel communication.

Benefits for Brand Engagement:
- √ Personalizes customer interactions, reinforcing brand values.
- √ Automates routine queries while keeping a human touch in complex situations.
- √ Builds a cohesive experience across platforms.

5. HubSpot Service Hub

HubSpot Service Hub integrates AI to improve customer support, offering tools like ticketing, chatbots, and automation. It helps brands deliver consistent and timely support while aligning with their core values and messaging.

Key Features:
- √ AI-powered chatbots for managing routine queries.
- √ Unified inbox for cross-channel support.
- √ Self-service knowledge base creation for customer empowerment.

Benefits for Brand Engagement:
- √ Increases response time while maintaining brand tone.
- √ Automates routine tasks, allowing human agents to focus on complex issues.

√ Strengthens brand trust by offering consistently excellent customer support.

6. Tidio

Tidio is an AI-powered live chat and chatbot solution designed for small and medium-sized businesses. It helps brands engage with customers in real time across websites, email, and social media, improving customer service and driving sales.

Key Features:
√ Live chat integration with AI-powered chatbots for 24/7 support.
√ Supports integration with popular e-commerce platforms like Shopify.
√ Customizable chatbots to match your brand's personality and tone.

Benefits for Brand Engagement:
√ Provides instant responses, keeping customers engaged and satisfied.
√ AI-driven solutions ensure consistent messaging across platforms.
√ Helps businesses reduce response times and improve customer satisfaction.

7. LivePerson

LivePerson is an AI-powered conversational platform that enhances customer engagement through real-time messaging and automation. It focuses on using AI to scale personalized customer interactions across digital channels.

Key Features:
√ AI-driven chatbots for messaging platforms (SMS, Facebook, WhatsApp, web chat).

- √ Integration with voice assistants like Alexa and Google Assistant.
- √ Automated lead qualification and customer support.

Benefits for Brand Engagement:
- √ Delivers real-time, personalized interactions that improve customer satisfaction.
- √ Consistent messaging across multiple channels keeps branding intact.
- √ Increases operational efficiency by automating repetitive customer service tasks.

AI tools like **ManyChat, Drift, Zendesk, Intercom, HubSpot Service Hub, Tidio,** and **LivePerson** allow businesses to maintain consistent and engaging customer service across multiple platforms. These tools not only enhance customer satisfaction but also help reinforce your brand messaging and build stronger, long-term relationships with your audience.

How AI-Powered Tools Enhance Brand Engagement
Through automation and personalization, you can ensure that your brand delivers seamless experiences that reflect your core values and identity.
- √ **Faster Response Times**: AI tools provide immediate answers to customer questions, reducing the frustration of long wait times and improving overall customer satisfaction.
- √ **Personalized Interactions**: By learning from previous interactions, AI chatbots can provide personalized responses and recommendations, making customers feel understood and valued.

- √ **24/7 Availability**: AI tools allow you to offer round-the-clock support, ensuring that your customers can get the help they need, whenever they need it.
- √ **Efficient Scaling**: AI-powered tools enable businesses to scale their customer service operations without increasing staff, making it easier to handle high volumes of inquiries.

This is Branding Example: Sephora
Sephora uses an AI chatbot on its website and mobile app to provide personalized beauty recommendations, answer customer questions, and even book in-store appointments. This chatbot allows Sephora to engage with customers in real-time, offering personalized support based on each user's preferences and needs.

AI-powered customer service tools allow your brand to be 'always on,' delivering personalized and responsive support that builds trust and keeps customers coming back. AI offers powerful tools that can enhance your branding strategy by delivering personalized experiences, analyzing customer sentiment, and improving customer service. As AI continues to evolve, brands that embrace these technologies will be better positioned to build stronger, more meaningful connections with their audience.

By leveraging AI-driven personalization, sentiment analysis, and AI-powered customer service, you can create a brand that not only meets the expectations of today's customers but also anticipates their needs and preferences. In the process, you'll build trust, increase loyalty, and boost your brand's currency in the marketplace.

CHAPTER 11
MEASURING BRAND SUCCESS

Building a strong brand is an ongoing journey, and just like any other aspect of business, your brand's success must be measured to ensure it's working effectively. Measuring your brand's reach and results gives you clear insights into how your audience perceives your brand, how well your efforts are paying off, and where improvements can be made. Without this feedback loop, it's impossible to know whether your branding strategies are resonating with your audience or if they need adjustment.

In this chapter, we'll explore the importance of tracking key metrics to measure your brand's success and ensure you're making the right impact. We'll dive into essential performance indicators like brand awareness, customer loyalty, and engagement, along with the tools and techniques that can help you measure your brand's performance in real-time. With a solid understanding of these metrics, you'll be able to refine your branding strategy, improve customer relationships, and ultimately drive long-term growth.

When it comes to measuring the success of your brand, the metrics you track will depend on your business goals. However, some key metrics are universally important for any brand looking to build a lasting relationship with its audience. These metrics help you gauge not just how many people are aware of your brand but also how they feel about it and whether they are loyal to your offerings. Let's take a closer look at the top three key metrics for tracking your brand's performance: brand awareness, customer loyalty, and engagement.

Expanding Brand Visibility: Measure Awareness and Reach

Brand awareness measures how well your audience knows and recognizes your brand. It's the foundation of branding because, without awareness, none of your other branding efforts matter. A high level of brand awareness means that people can easily identify your brand, know what it stands for, and recall it when they think of your industry or product category.

If people aren't aware of your brand, they can't engage with it or buy from you. Brand awareness is the first step in the customer journey—it's the spark that ignites interest and consideration. The more recognizable your brand is, the easier it is to attract new customers and retain existing ones.

Tracking Brand Awareness
√ **Impressions and Reach**: Track how many people have been exposed to your brand through social media, advertising campaigns, and website visits. Metrics like impressions (how often your content is

viewed) and reach (the number of unique viewers) give you a sense of how far your brand is spreading.

√ **Direct and Organic Traffic**: Website analytics tools like Google Analytics can show how many people are visiting your website directly (by typing in your URL) or organically (through search engines). A high level of direct traffic suggests strong brand recognition.

√ **Branded Search Volume**: Monitor the number of people searching for your brand name online. An increase in branded search volume indicates that more people are aware of your brand and actively seeking you out.

√ **Social Media Mentions**: Use social media listening tools to track how often people mention your brand on platforms like Twitter, Instagram, and Facebook. The more mentions your brand receives, the higher its awareness.

This is Branding Example: Nike
Nike's brand awareness is off the charts. The iconic swoosh logo is instantly recognizable worldwide, even without the brand's name attached to it. Nike has built a brand that's synonymous with athleticism, innovation, and motivation. Their brand awareness campaigns, such as their "Just Do It" slogan, have made the brand unforgettable to millions of people.

Author's Insight
Brand awareness is the first step toward brand success. If people don't know you exist, they can't connect with you. The more recognizable your brand, the more opportunities you have to build lasting relationships.

Building Brand Advocates: Track Customer Loyalty
Customer loyalty measures how consistently your customers choose your brand over competitors. It reflects the strength of the relationship between your brand and your audience. Loyal customers are those who repeatedly purchase from you, advocate for your brand, and are less likely to switch to a competitor, even when alternatives are available.

Loyal customers are invaluable to your brand's growth. Not only do they generate repeat business, but they also act as brand ambassadors, spreading positive word-of-mouth and driving new customer acquisition. Studies show that acquiring a new customer is significantly more expensive than retaining an existing one, so building customer loyalty is crucial for sustainable growth.

Key Factors to Measuring Customer Loyalty
Repeat Purchase Rate: This metric tracks how often customers return to make another purchase. A high repeat purchase rate indicates that customers are satisfied with your product or service and choose your brand consistently.

Customer Lifetime Value (CLV): CLV measures the total revenue a customer is expected to generate for your brand throughout their entire relationship with you. The higher the CLV, the more loyal your customers are and the more value they bring to your business over time.

Net Promoter Score (NPS): NPS is a popular metric that measures how likely your customers are to recommend your brand to others. It's a great indicator of customer satisfaction and loyalty. Customers are asked to rate their likelihood of recommending your brand on a scale of 0 to 10, and NPS calculates the percentage of promoters (those who score 9-10) minus the percentage of detractors (those who score 0-6).

Churn Rate: This metric measures the percentage of customers who stop doing business with you over a given period. A low churn rate is a good sign that your brand is successfully retaining customers and building loyalty.

This is Branding Example: Starbucks
Starbucks has built a loyal customer base through its Starbucks Rewards loyalty program. The app-based program encourages repeat purchases by offering points for every dollar spent, which can be redeemed for free drinks and other rewards. This incentivizes customers to keep coming back, creating long-term loyalty and higher customer lifetime value.

Author's Insight

Customer loyalty is earned through trust and consistency. Loyal customers are not just repeat buyers—they're your brand's advocates, spreading the word and driving growth organically.

Driving Meaningful Interactions: Gauge Audience Engagement
Engagement measures how actively your audience interacts with your brand. It goes beyond passive awareness to track how much your audience is participating in conversations, sharing your content, and responding to your messaging. Engagement is a crucial metric because it indicates how well your brand is

connecting with its audience and how invested your customers are in your brand.

High engagement means that your brand resonates with your audience. When people engage with your content—whether by liking, commenting, sharing, or clicking on a link—it shows that they're paying attention and are interested in what your brand has to say. Engaged customers are more likely to make a purchase, share your brand with others, and become loyal supporters.

How to Measure Engagement

Social Media Interactions: Track likes, comments, shares, retweets, and direct messages on social media platforms. The higher the engagement, the more relevant and interesting your content is to your audience.

Click-Through Rates (CTR): Monitor the percentage of people who click on links in your emails, ads, or social media posts. A high CTR indicates that your content is compelling and prompts action.

Time Spent on Site: Use website analytics tools to track how long visitors spend on your website. The longer they stay, the more engaged they are with your content.

Content Shares: Track how often your blog posts, videos, or other content are shared across social media or through direct links. Shares are a strong indicator of engagement because they show that people find your content valuable enough to pass along to others.

This is Branding Example: Glossier

Glossier, a beauty brand known for its direct-to-consumer model, has built a highly engaged online community. Glossier's customers frequently share their experiences with the brand on social media, tagging Glossier in posts and participating in discussions about beauty and skincare. This engagement has been key to Glossier's growth, as the brand relies heavily on word-of-mouth and user-generated content to build awareness and trust.

Author's Insight

Engagement is where your brand's personality shines. It's not just about talking—it's about starting a conversation that resonates with your audience and keeps them coming back for more.

Tools and Techniques for Measuring Success

Tracking brand performance across key metrics requires the right tools and techniques. From social media platforms to customer feedback surveys, there are numerous tools available to help you measure brand awareness, customer loyalty, and engagement. Below are some of the most effective tools for tracking your brand's success and how to use them.

1. Google Analytics

What It Does: Google Analytics is a free tool that tracks website traffic, user behavior, and conversions. It provides insights into how visitors interact with your website, how they found you, and what actions they take once they arrive.

How to Use It: Use Google Analytics to monitor website traffic, bounce rates, session duration, and conversion rates. You can also track the effectiveness of your marketing campaigns by analyzing referral sources and how they contribute to overall traffic and engagement.

2. Sprout Social

What It Does: Sprout Social is a social media management tool that helps you track engagement across platforms like Facebook, Instagram, Twitter, and LinkedIn. It provides detailed analytics on social media performance, including follower growth, engagement rates, and audience demographics.

How to Use It: Use Sprout Social to track social media mentions, interactions, and brand sentiment. The platform also allows you to schedule posts and monitor engagement in real-time, giving you a clear picture of how your audience is interacting with your brand.

3. HubSpot

What It Does: HubSpot is an all-in-one CRM, marketing, and sales tool that offers analytics on customer interactions, website performance, and campaign effectiveness. HubSpot's reporting dashboard lets you track customer lifecycle stages and marketing KPIs.

How to Use It: Use HubSpot to measure customer loyalty through metrics like repeat purchases and customer lifetime value. HubSpot also tracks lead generation, email marketing performance, and customer engagement, making it a great tool for holistic brand measurement.

4. Net Promoter Score (NPS) Surveys

What It Does: NPS surveys measure customer satisfaction and loyalty by asking customers how likely they are to recommend your brand to others, using a scale of 0 to 10.

How to Use It: Send NPS surveys via email to gather direct feedback from customers. Analyze the scores to determine your percentage of promoters, passives, and detractors, then use the feedback to improve your customer experience.

5. Brandwatch

What It Does: Brandwatch is a social listening tool that tracks brand mentions across the web and social media, giving you insights into how people are talking about your brand and the sentiment behind those conversations.

How to Use It: Use Brandwatch to monitor brand sentiment, track the volume of brand mentions, and analyze customer feedback. The tool helps you understand how your audience feels about your brand and what issues or trends are influencing their perception.

Measuring your brand's success is an essential step in building a strong, lasting presence in the market. By tracking key metrics like brand awareness, customer loyalty, and engagement, you can gain valuable insights into how your audience perceives your brand and how effectively your strategies are working.

With the right tools and techniques, you can refine your branding efforts, optimize customer experiences, and strengthen your relationship with your audience. Remember, measuring success isn't a one-time task—it's an ongoing process that allows you to continuously improve and grow.

CHAPTER 12
TROUBLESHOOTING COMMON
BRANDING ISSUES

No matter how strong your brand is, challenges are inevitable. Even well-established brands occasionally encounter issues where their messaging falls flat, their audience engagement drops, or they face negative feedback. These challenges, while daunting, offer valuable learning opportunities and can strengthen your brand in the long run-if handled correctly. Knowing how to troubleshoot common branding issues can help you navigate crises, refine your approach, and ensure that your brand remains strong and resilient.

In this chapter, we'll explore some of the most common branding issues businesses face and provide actionable solutions for overcoming them. Whether your brand isn't resonating with your audience, you're dealing with negative feedback, or it's time to refresh your identity, this chapter will give you the tools to get your brand back on track without losing sight of your core values.

What To Do When Your Brand Isn't Resonating: Understand The Problem

One of the most frustrating challenges for any business is realizing that your brand isn't resonating with your target audience. This can manifest in various ways-lower sales, disengaged customers, or a lack of traction on social media or marketing efforts. The key to solving this issue is identifying where the disconnect is happening. Are your messaging and visuals failing to communicate your brand's value? Is your audience unclear on what you stand for? Or is there a misalignment between your offerings and what your target market needs?

How To Address It

Revisit your target audience: one of the most common reasons brands fail to resonate is that they've lost touch with their audience. Market conditions change, and so do consumer preferences. Start by conducting market research to reassess your audience's current needs, pain points, and preferences. Are you targeting the right demographic? Has your audience evolved in ways your brand hasn't adapted to? Make sure your messaging and offerings align with what your audience values today.

Audit your brand messaging: take a deep look at your messaging across all platforms. Is it clear, consistent, and compelling? Are you effectively communicating your brand's unique selling proposition (USP)? Sometimes, brands drift away from their core message as they grow. Simplify and refocus your messaging to emphasize the aspects of your brand that resonate most with your audience.

Improve customer experience: if your brand isn't resonating, it may be because the customer experience doesn't live up to expectations. Whether it's website navigation, product quality, or customer service, every touchpoint matters. Conduct customer feedback surveys and listen to your customers' experiences to identify areas where you can improve.

Engage in direct conversations: reach out to your customers directly, whether through surveys, focus groups, or social media engagement. Ask what they like about your brand and where they feel there's room for improvement. Genuine dialogue with your audience can reveal hidden gaps in your strategy and offer insights for reconnecting.

This Is Branding Example: Pepsi's 2017 Ad Campaign

In 2017, Pepsi launched a controversial ad featuring Kendall Jenner that attempted to align the brand with social justice movements. The ad was widely criticized for being tone-deaf and trivializing important issues, leading to a disconnect with their audience. Pepsi pulled the ad and issued a public apology, acknowledging that they had missed the mark. This example highlights the importance of staying in touch with your audience and avoiding messaging that feels inauthentic or out of touch with current social issues.

How To Handle Negative Feedback Professionally: Understand the Impact

Negative feedback is inevitable for any brand, no matter how successful. Whether it's a bad product review, a social media complaint, or a public relations crisis, how you respond can make or break your reputation. Handling negative feedback professionally and thoughtfully is essential for turning a potential setback into an opportunity to strengthen your brand.

Steps To Handling Negative Feedback

Acknowledge The Feedback: the worst thing a brand can do is ignore or dismiss negative feedback. Acknowledge the customer's concern publicly, whether it's on social media, a review platform, or through direct communication. A simple, "thank you for bringing this to our attention" shows that you're listening and taking the issue seriously.

Respond quickly and thoughtfully: timeliness is key when dealing with negative feedback. The faster you respond, the more control you retain over the narrative. However, ensure that your response is thoughtful and not rushed. Offer a genuine apology where necessary and explain the steps your brand is taking to address the issue.

Take responsibility: owning up to mistakes is one of the most effective ways to rebuild trust. If the issue was your brand's fault, admit it. Customers appreciate transparency, and taking responsibility shows that your brand values integrity.

Offer A Solution: acknowledging the problem is important, but offering a solution is what will truly make the difference. Whether it's a refund, replacement, or another form of compensation, let the customer know how you plan to resolve the issue. Publicly demonstrating that you are willing to make things right reinforces a positive image of your brand.

Turn negative feedback into an opportunity: negative feedback can reveal blind spots in your business. Use it as an opportunity to improve your products, services, or customer experience. Engage with the customer by asking for further details or suggestions on how you can improve, and then follow through on those improvements.

This Is Branding Example: United Airlines' Response To The Passenger Removal Incident

In 2017, united airlines faced a public relations crisis after a passenger was forcibly removed from a flight. The airline initially downplayed the incident, referring to it as an "overbooking situation," which only fueled public outrage. After widespread backlash, united issued a more heartfelt apology, admitted fault, and made policy changes to prevent similar situations in the future. This incident serves as a reminder that swift, honest responses are crucial when dealing with negative feedback.

Refreshing Your Brand Without Losing Its Identity

Even the most successful brands need to refresh their identity from time to time. Market trends change, customer preferences evolve, and new competitors emerge-forcing brands to stay fresh and relevant. A brand refresh can involve updating your logo, revisiting your messaging, or modernizing your overall aesthetic. However, it's essential to do this without losing the core identity and values that have made your brand successful.

Steps To Refresh Your Brand Effectively

Start with your brand's core values: before making any changes, revisit your brand's mission, vision, and values. These foundational elements should remain consistent, even as you refresh other aspects of your brand. For example, if your brand was built on sustainability, make sure your refreshed identity reflects that commitment, even if the look and feel change.

Evaluate what needs to change: not every aspect of your brand needs a refresh. Conduct a brand audit to identify which elements-such as your logo, typography, color palette, or messaging-are outdated or no longer resonating with your audience. Focus on the areas that will have the most impact without confusing your customers.

Communicate the change: a brand refresh should never come as a surprise to your audience. Communicate the reasons for the refresh and what it means for your customers. Let them know that while your brand's look or feel may be changing, your values and commitment to them remain the same. Transparency helps avoid alienating your loyal customer base.

Involve your audience: consider involving your customers in the refresh process. Gather feedback on potential design or messaging changes through surveys, focus groups, or even social media polls. Involving your audience makes them feel like part of the process and ensures that the refresh aligns with their expectations.

Gradual vs. Total overhaul: depending on the scale of change required, decide whether a gradual refresh or a total overhaul is more appropriate. A gradual approach (small changes over time) allows customers to adapt to the new identity slowly. In contrast, a total overhaul can make a bold statement but should only be used when your brand needs significant changes.

This Is Branding Example: Dunkin' Rebrand
In 2018, Dunkin' (formerly Dunkin' donuts) decided to drop "donuts" from its name as part of a brand refresh to reflect its broader focus on beverages and quick-service food. While the name and logo were updated, the core elements that customers loved-its coffee and fast service-remained intact. Dunkin' was able to modernize its brand without alienating its loyal customer base, showing how a refresh can be done while staying true to the brand's essence.

Every brand encounters challenges, whether it's losing resonance with customers, dealing with negative feedback, or undergoing a refresh. The key to overcoming these challenges lies in being proactive, transparent, and staying true to your brand's core identity. By understanding your audience, engaging with feedback, and knowing when and how to refresh your brand, you can turn potential issues into opportunities for growth and long-term success.

Strong brands aren't those that avoid challenges-they're the ones that face them head-on and emerge even stronger. With the strategies outlined in this chapter, you'll be well-equipped to troubleshoot common branding issues and keep your brand thriving.

CHAPTER 13
DELULU IS THE SOLULU

In 2024, the playful phrase "Delulu is the Solulu" (short for "Delusion is the Solution") has become the cultural shorthand for embracing aspirational thinking and believing in bold, almost fantastical possibilities. When I first heard it, I was taken aback. But as I reflected on the concept, it started to make perfect sense to my analytical yet creative brain. From a branding perspective, this phrase beautifully captures the essence of **how effective branding** allows people to "get lost" in a brand—creating a world where customers emotionally connect with the vision, dreams, and lifestyle the brand represents.

I had the privilege of discussing this with a client I deeply admire: the CEO of one of the nation's leading catering companies. His support for our agency over the years has been invaluable. At the beginning of 2024, he reached out to me with a challenge—how could they bring their brand more in tune with the times through digital marketing? He wanted to reimagine how they could engage a wider audience while rekindling connections with their loyal customer base to drive growth in the ever-evolving marketplace.

When we sat down to discuss, I introduced "Delulu is the Solulu" as a framework for their digital strategy. I explained that in today's world, brands need to tap into bold, imaginative thinking to capture attention, create emotional connections, and build customer loyalty. It's not just about selling a service or product anymore—it's about creating an experience, a lifestyle, and a vision that resonates deeply with people.

With this approach, we strategized how the company could reposition the brand to re-engage their existing audience and capture new segments through digital storytelling, creative campaigns, and aspirational messaging. It was a testament to his leadership that he was open to this modern way of thinking in seeking to ultimately drive their business into the future. This chapter is dedicated to my client, a true visionary and leader who continuously seeks to evolve, innovate, and inspire— thank you for your support and trust in our partnership.

Brands that are able to embrace this philosophy can create **immersive experiences**, many of which we've seen playout on social media very effectively in 2024. These are experiences that blur the lines between reality and aspiration. When done right, branding can be so compelling that it transforms ordinary products or services, even people into **symbols of identity, aspiration, and lifestyle**, driving customers to want to dive deeper into the brand's world.

Here's how this "Delulu" mindset plays out in branding:

Visionary Branding: Selling A Dream, Not Just A Product

At its core, "Delulu is the Solulu" represents the idea of selling **aspirations** rather than merely products. Effective branding helps customers believe they are buying into a lifestyle or dream. This can be seen in brands that create an emotional world customers want to immerse themselves in.

This is Branding Example: Oura Ring

Oura Ring, a leading health-tech wearable brand, goes beyond selling a fitness tracker. It sells the vision of optimal health and self-awareness, positioning itself as a tool for biohackers, wellness enthusiasts, and anyone who wants to take control of their health. By emphasizing its cutting-edge ability to track sleep, recovery, and overall health in an intimate, data-driven way, Oura Ring invites its users into a lifestyle of self-optimization. The brand doesn't just promote health metrics; it sells the belief that you can live better, longer, and more mindfully with the right tools. Customers aren't just buying a ring—they're buying the **aspirational belief in holistic wellness**.

Immersive Experiences: Customers Want To Get Lost In

Just like "Delulu is the Solulu" suggests getting lost in a dream, effective branding creates a **world** customers can mentally and emotionally dive into. It's about creating an environment where the brand's story and identity are so captivating that customers feel part of something bigger than a product—part of a **movement or culture**.

This is Branding Example: Roblox

Roblox has successfully built an immersive virtual world that captivates users across all demographics. In 2024, the gaming platform evolved into a **metaverse-style ecosystem**, where users don't just play games—they create and live digital lives, collaborate, and experience entertainment events. Roblox sells the idea of **limitless creativity** and the belief that anyone can create, play, and even earn a living within their virtual universe. The brand's immersive nature draws people in, making them feel like they're part of a constantly evolving world where their imagination can thrive without limits.

Branding As Belief: The Power Of Delusional Thinking

The idea that "Delulu is the Solulu" can also apply to **how brands inspire belief** in the impossible or improbable. Successful brands convince customers to believe in something they may not have considered before. This level of belief can border on "delusional" in the sense that the brand is able to sell not just a product, but an **idea that transcends reality**- something customers feel emotionally attached to, even if it seems larger than life.

This is Branding Example: SpaceX

SpaceX, under Elon Musk's leadership, has moved beyond being just a company focused on space exploration. It has transformed into a brand that represents **humanity's bold future**—one where space travel and multi-planetary living are realities. SpaceX sells more than rockets; it sells the belief that we, as a species, can transcend Earth and explore new frontiers. This bold vision captivates dreamers, scientists, and explorers, making them emotionally invested in a brand that represents **limitless possibility**. Customers who follow SpaceX are deeply connected to the belief that humanity's future lies in the stars, making the brand aspirational on a global scale.

Brands That Craft Emotional Attachment
Brands that embrace the "Delulu is the Solulu" mindset **connect with people emotionally**. They create such strong emotional bonds that customers begin to associate the brand with their own identity. People don't just use the brand—they see themselves reflected in it.

This is Branding Example: Glossier
Glossier, a beauty brand built on simplicity and customer connection, has continued to foster an **inclusive beauty community** where customers feel seen, heard, and represented. In 2024, Glossier's success stems from its ability to **humanize beauty**—focusing not just on how products make you look, but how they make you feel. By emphasizing individuality, personal care, and self-expression, Glossier invites its customers into a community where everyone's beauty journey is celebrated. The brand uses user-generated content, real customer stories, and a personal touch to make its products feel like more than cosmetics—they become an extension of the customer's identity.

The Power of Fandom: Cult Brands as The Ultimate "Delulu" Experience
Some brands go so far as to create **cult-like followings**, where customers become brand evangelists, spreading the brand's vision with an almost religious fervor. These brands embody the "Delulu is the Solulu" concept by creating an entire lifestyle or belief system around their products, with customers willingly losing themselves in the brand's world.

This is Branding Example: Peloton

Peloton has successfully cultivated a dedicated **cult following** around its fitness platform. More than just a stationary bike company, Peloton has created a community of fitness enthusiasts who believe in the brand's message of empowerment, inclusivity, and achieving your best self. In 2024, Peloton's branding has evolved to emphasize community, connection, and mental resilience. Customers aren't just buying a piece of exercise equipment—they're joining a **movement** of like-minded people committed to pushing their limits, supporting each other, and sharing in victories, big and small. Peloton's instructors have become motivational figures, making the brand's ecosystem feel like an uplifting, personal fitness journey.

"Delulu is the Solulu" captures the power of brands that create immersive, aspirational worlds where customers get emotionally lost. This approach transforms a simple transaction into an emotional journey, making the brand an indispensable part of the customer's life. When customers buy into a brand that makes them feel part of something bigger—whether it's a dream, a movement, or a transformation—they aren't just buying products. They're engaging with a belief system, and that's where the real power of effective branding lies.

At this stage of the book, I want to take a moment to congratulate you on making it this far. You've committed to understanding the essential elements of branding, and now it's time to reflect on the core principles that will elevate your brand to the next level. By reaching this point, you've gained the knowledge and insights to build a brand that people love, feel invested in, and that can stand the test of time. Branding is the heart and soul of your business. It's what connects you with your customers, sets you apart from the competition, and fosters long-term loyalty. You've learned that creating a brand goes far beyond a logo or slogan—it's about telling a compelling story, building trust, emotionally connecting with your audience, and delivering consistent value at every touchpoint.

Whether you're in the early stages of building a business or seeking to strengthen an established brand, I hope this book has provided clarity to the most important principles of branding. From understanding the deeper purpose behind your brand to crafting an emotional connection with your audience, each strategy plays a vital role in creating a brand that resonates and stands out.

Here is a recap of the essential takeaways:
The Shortcut to Mastering Branding Strategies
Branding can feel like a complex process, but at its core, it's about understanding your business, your audience, and how to connect the two in a way that's authentic and engaging. Let's take a moment to recap the most critical elements of building a strong brand, so you can walk away with actionable steps that will drive real results.

1. **Know Your 'Why'**
   At the center of every successful brand is a clear and compelling 'why.' Your brand's purpose should reflect the passion, mission, and values that guide your business. Understanding why your brand exists—and clearly communicating that to your audience—creates an emotional connection that builds loyalty and trust. Whether your 'why' is based on solving a problem, driving innovation, or

making a difference in the world, it needs to be front and center in all your branding efforts.

2. **Create a Consistent Brand Identity**
Consistency is the foundation of a strong brand. From your logo and color palette to your messaging and tone of voice, every element of your brand should be cohesive and easily recognizable. Customers trust brands that deliver a consistent experience across all touchpoints, whether they're interacting with your website, social media, packaging, or customer service team. Consistent branding reinforces who you are and helps you build a memorable presence in the market.

3. **Tell a Story that Resonates**
People don't just buy products or services; they buy stories and experiences. Effective storytelling humanizes your brand and makes it relatable. Your brand's story should communicate your journey, the challenges you've overcome, and the value you bring to your customers. Be authentic and transparent in your storytelling, and don't be afraid to show vulnerability. It's these human elements that create a deeper connection with your audience.

4. **Engage with Your Audience**
Building a brand people love means creating opportunities for ongoing engagement. Whether through social media, email newsletters, or face-to-face interactions, regularly communicate with your audience in ways that make them feel valued and heard. Listen to their feedback, respond to

their needs, and show appreciation for their loyalty. Engagement isn't a one-time effort—it's an ongoing conversation that strengthens your relationship with customers over time.

5. **Leverage Personalization and Technology**
   Today's consumers expect personalized experiences, and AI tools have made it easier than ever to deliver them. Use customer data to tailor your offerings, messages, and recommendations. Personalization makes customers feel valued and increases their likelihood of becoming long-term advocates for your brand. Whether through personalized email campaigns, targeted ads, or tailored product suggestions, technology allows you to connect with customers in ways that feel unique and relevant to them.

6. **Measure, Adapt, and Improve**
   Branding isn't a set-it-and-forget-it strategy. As market conditions and consumer behaviors change, your brand needs to evolve. Regularly measure key metrics like brand awareness, customer loyalty, and engagement to track how well your branding efforts are performing. Use tools like Google Analytics, social media insights, and customer surveys to gather data and refine your strategy. Brands that succeed over the long term are those that stay flexible and continuously adapt to meet the needs of their audience.

Building a brand is a journey, and like all journeys, it comes with its fair share of challenges, roadblocks, and uncertainties. But the reward is worth it. A strong brand is more than just a marketing tool—it's an asset that drives trust, loyalty, and long-term growth. Your brand is a reflection of your values, your vision, and your passion for what you do, and when done right, it has the power to transform your business.

As an entrepreneur, you'll face ups and downs but remember that every step forward brings you closer to your goals. Branding is a process, not a destination, and the key to success is consistency, patience, and perseverance. Don't be afraid to take risks, to experiment with new ideas, and to make mistakes. Each challenge presents an opportunity to learn, grow, and refine your approach.

Here are some thoughts to carry with you as you move forward in your entrepreneurial journey:

1. **Believe in Your Brand**
   Confidence is key. If you believe in your brand, others will too. Stay true to your vision, and don't let fear of failure hold you back. Every successful brand started with a leap of faith, and yours will be no different.

2. **Stay Authentic**
   Authenticity builds trust. Customers can sense when a brand is being genuine, and they respond to that authenticity by becoming loyal advocates. Stay true to your brand's values and mission, and never compromise them in pursuit of short-term gains.

3. **Be Resilient**
   The entrepreneurial journey is not linear. There will be setbacks, but the most successful entrepreneurs are those who keep going despite

the obstacles. Resilience is the key to long-term success. Keep pushing forward, and never give up on your brand.

4. **Celebrate Small Wins**
   Building a brand takes time, so celebrate the small victories along the way. Whether it's hitting a milestone in social media followers, launching a successful product, or receiving positive customer feedback, these wins are proof that you're on the right track.

A successful brand is not built overnight. It requires careful planning, thoughtful execution, and ongoing commitment. But by focusing on the fundamentals—knowing your 'why,' creating consistency, telling authentic stories, engaging with your audience, and adapting to Change—you can create a brand that people love.

Your brand is a living, evolving entity that reflects your passion, purpose, and the value you bring to the world. Every step you take, every decision you make, is an opportunity to strengthen your brand and build deeper connections with your audience. Stay dedicated, stay authentic, and most importantly, stay true to the vision that inspired you to start this journey in the first place.

As someone who has walked the entrepreneurial path, I know firsthand how challenging and rewarding the journey of building a brand can be. There will be days when the road seems long, and the obstacles feel insurmountable— but it's during those times that your dedication and passion for your brand will make all the difference. The most successful brands aren't always the biggest or the flashiest—they're the ones that connect with people on a deep, emotional level. They're authentic, they're consistent, and they stay true to their core values no matter what. Your brand has the potential to do the same. Remember, building a brand isn't about perfection. It's about progress, growth, and connection.

Keep pushing forward, keep learning, and most importantly, stay true to what inspired you to create your brand in the first place. You've got everything you need to build something incredible—now go make it happen.

— **Karee Laing**

CHAPTER 14
RESOURCES TO JUST GET STARTED

Now that you've explored the ins and outs of branding—what it is, how to create it, and how to keep it strong—the question remains: What's next? With the knowledge and strategies you've gained, you're ready to take action and lead your business toward a brand that's not only powerful but enduring. It's time to apply these principles, make bold moves, and guide your brand in the right direction, ensuring it resonates with your audience and continues to grow.

Understand that branding is a continuous process of evolving, refining, and engaging with your audience. Whether you're starting from scratch or looking to elevate your existing brand, the steps you take from this point forward will set the foundation for your long-term success.

Now, let's look at a few actionable steps you can take after reading this book; these are practical ways to start implementing branding strategies right away, and additional resources to continue your branding education.

Let's turn what you've learned into a tangible plan that will drive real results for your business. **JUST GET STARTED**

Steps to Take After Reading This Book -
Completing this book has given you a solid understanding of what branding is and how it can shape the future of your business. Now it's time to translate that knowledge into action.

Here's a step-by-step guide to ensure you're moving forward with purpose and focus:

Audit Your Current Brand
The first step is to evaluate where your brand currently stands. Conduct a full brand audit to assess your existing messaging, visual identity, customer perceptions, and market positioning. Are you clearly communicating your values and unique selling proposition (USP)? Is your branding consistent across all touchpoints—website, social media, packaging, etc.? Identifying areas of weakness or opportunities for improvement will provide clarity on what needs immediate attention.

1. **Define or Refine Your Brand Identity**
   If your brand identity isn't clearly defined, this is your priority. Revisit your brand's mission, vision, values, and core messaging to ensure they align with your long-term goals and the needs of your target audience. For those with an established brand identity, this is the time to refine it, ensuring that it's up to date and still resonates with the market. Use the tools and strategies outlined in earlier chapters to ensure your identity reflects the

essence of your business and stands out from the competition.

2. **Set Measurable Goals**

   To stay on track, set specific, measurable goals for your branding efforts. These goals could range from increasing brand awareness, improving customer engagement, or building a more loyal customer base. Be clear about what success looks like for your brand and how you'll measure it. For example, you could aim to increase social media engagement by 20% over the next quarter or see a rise in customer referrals by the end of the year.

3. **Develop a Brand Strategy Roadmap**

   Now that you've assessed your brand and set goals, create a strategic roadmap that outlines how you will achieve them. Break down your larger goals into actionable steps, such as launching a brand refresh, improving customer experience, or expanding your content marketing efforts. Assign timelines, resources, and responsibilities to each task to ensure you stay focused and on track.

4. **Engage Your Team**

   Branding is a team effort. If you have employees or partners, make sure everyone is aligned with the brand's vision and values. Conduct internal branding workshops or training to ensure your team knows how to communicate and embody your brand, both internally and externally.

5. **Start Small but Stay Consistent**
    Branding doesn't need to be a huge, overwhelming effort at first. Start small by improving one aspect of your brand—whether that's updating your website's messaging, refining your logo, or launching a new social media campaign. The key is consistency. Even small changes, when applied consistently, can lead to big results over time.

Start Implementing Branding Strategies Today

Implementing your branding strategies doesn't have to wait. There are several actions you can take right away to start building a stronger brand presence. Here's how to start putting your branding knowledge into action today:

1. **Update Your Visual Identity**
    One of the easiest ways to start implementing your branding strategies is by refreshing your brand's visual elements. Whether it's updating your logo, choosing a new color palette, or refining your typography, your visual identity is often the first point of contact with customers. Ensure that these elements are consistent across all platforms, from your website and social media to your physical packaging or storefront.

2. **Create a Content Plan**
    Content is one of the most powerful tools for building and communicating your brand. Develop a content strategy that aligns with your brand's voice and values. Whether it's blog posts, videos, or social media updates, create content that resonates with your target audience and reinforces your brand's message. For example, if a core value

is sustainability, then create content around eco-friendly practices, industry trends, or customer stories that highlight your brand's commitment to sustainability.

3. **Engage with Your Audience**
   Start connecting with your customers right away by engaging with them on social media, responding to feedback, and asking for input. Whether you're replying to comments, posting polls, or encouraging user-generated content, these small interactions build trust and loyalty. Remember, it's not just about talking—it's about listening to what your audience has to say and responding to their needs.

4. **Implement Personalization**
   Use customer data to begin personalizing experiences. Whether it's through targeted emails, personalized product recommendations, or tailored offers, personalization makes customers feel valued and understood. AI tools like HubSpot, Mailchimp, or customer relationship management (CRM) systems can help you start personalizing interactions based on customer preferences and behavior.

5. **Evaluate Your Customer Journey**
   Take time to map out your customer journey—from the first point of contact to post-purchase follow-up. Identify areas where you can improve the customer experience and ensure that each touchpoint reflects your brand's values. Do customers feel supported? Are you building long-

term relationships rather than just focusing on single transactions? Improving the customer journey can lead to higher satisfaction and loyalty.

Utilize Additional Resources for Ongoing Branding Education

Branding is an evolving field, and staying current with the latest trends and strategies is crucial for long-term success. Below are some recommended resources for ongoing learning and development to help you keep your brand fresh, relevant, and growing.

1. **Books on Branding**
   - *Building a StoryBrand* by Donald Miller: A fave of mine, this book focuses on how to clarify your brand's message through story-telling, ensuring that customers understand and connect with your brand.
   - *Start with Why* by Simon Sinek: A powerful read for understanding the importance of defining your brand's purpose and leading with your "why."
   - *Made to Stick* by Chip Heath and Dan Heath: Learn how to create messaging that sticks with your audience and makes your brand memorable.

2. **Online Courses and Workshops**
   - *Skillshare:* Offers courses on branding, marketing, and design to help you refine your skills and keep your branding strategies sharp.
   - *HubSpot Academy:* HubSpot provides free courses on content marketing, customer

engagement, and brand building. Their certifications are especially useful for business owners looking to deepen their marketing and branding expertise.

- o *Coursera*: Coursera has a range of courses, including "Brand Management: Aligning Business, Brand, and Behavior" from the University of London, which dives deep into managing and sustaining a strong brand.

3. **Branding and Marketing Podcasts**
   - o ***The GaryVee Audio Experience***: Gary Vaynerchuk's podcast is packed with practical advice on building brands, creating content, and leveraging digital platforms for growth.
   - o ***The Futur with Chris Do***: A fantastic resource for creative entrepreneurs and designers, offering insights into brand strategy, design, and marketing.
   - o ***Marketing School with Neil Patel and Eric Siu***: This daily podcast provides actionable tips on digital marketing, SEO, and branding that you can implement immediately.

4. **Branding Blogs and Newsletters**
   - o ***Branding Strategy Insider***: A blog dedicated to in-depth discussions on brand strategy, positioning, and innovation.
   - o ***The Dieline***: A leading packaging design blog that showcases creative packaging trends, branding, and sustainability in design.

- o **AdAge**: Offers insights into marketing trends, advertising campaigns, and brand success stories from leading global brands.

5. **Networking and Mentorship**
   - o **Join Branding Communities**: Consider joining branding or marketing-focused online communities such as LinkedIn groups, Reddit communities, or specialized forums. There is also networking with other industry professionals that can give you fresh perspectives and support as you refine your branding efforts.

   - o **Attend Industry Conferences**: Look for conferences that focus on branding, marketing, or business growth. Events like Adobe MAX, INBOUND, or Brand Manage Camp provide valuable insights into emerging trends, best practices, and opportunities for learning from industry leaders.

Now that you've completed this book, you have the foundation to create, maintain, and grow a strong brand that resonates with your customers and drives success. Whether you're auditing your current brand, refreshing your identity, or building from the ground up, the strategies in this book will help you stay on track.

Your brand is your most valuable asset—it's the connection between your business and your customers. By taking action now, you'll set your business up for long-term success, build trust with your audience, and differentiate yourself in a crowded marketplace.

Remember, the most important part of branding is consistency and authenticity. Keep evolving, keep learning, and keep refining your approach. The steps you take today will shape the future of your brand and its impact on the world.

CHAPTER 15
FINAL THOUGHTS: THIS IS BRANDING

When you first saw the cover of this book, what did you feel? Was it curiosity? A sense of intrigue? Maybe it struck you as bold, unconventional, and just a little different. Whatever the reaction, it made you stop, take a second look, and want to know more. That is branding.

Just as the cover draws you in with a visual statement that speaks directly to something in you, great branding does the same. It's the ability to capture attention, evoke emotion, and create curiosity—all in an instant. But it doesn't stop there. True branding delivers on that initial spark by providing substance, value, and meaning. It keeps you engaged and connected long after the first impression.

Your brand, like this cover, should be more than just an eye-catching design—it should make a statement about who you are, what you stand for, and why people should care. It's about being bold, standing out, and inviting others into a story that feels uniquely yours. When someone sees your brand for the first time, they should feel what you want them to feel—whether that's excitement, trust, or inspiration. It's about creating an emotional connection that compels them to take a step closer, to learn more, to believe in what you're offering.

The essence of branding is boldness with purpose. It's about not being afraid to be different, to push boundaries, to captivate an audience in ways they weren't expecting. The cover of this book is an extension of who I am as a marketer and a branding expert—bold, eclectic, unapologetic, and deeply committed to challenging the norm. I've designed this book, inside and out, to reflect what I teach: that branding is about leaving a lasting impression, one that doesn't fade with time but instead grows stronger.

So, as you finish reading, I invite you to think about how you can create that same feeling of curiosity and connection with your brand. How can you make someone stop, notice, and think, "This is different. I need to know more?"
Because at the end of the day, that is branding. Bold, authentic, and unforgettable.

And that's exactly what you have the power to create.

ADDITIONAL RESOURCES

Additional Resources for Branding Success
In addition to the strategies and insights covered in this book, here are some additional resources that can deepen your understanding of branding and help you build a stronger, more impactful brand. These books, tools, platforms, and communities offer practical knowledge and applications to complement the concepts covered in *This Is Branding*.

BOOKS AND READING RESOURCES
1. **Building a StoryBrand by Donald Miller**
   - √ Learn how to clarify your brand's message using a proven storytelling framework. Miller provides a step-by-step guide to creating a narrative that connects with customers on a deeper level.
2. **Start with Why by Simon Sinek**
   - √ Sinek explores how purpose-driven branding inspires loyalty and long-term success. Understanding your "why" helps create a brand that connects emotionally with your audience.

3. **Brand Gap by Marty Neumeier**
   - √ This book provides insight into the gap between brand strategy and execution. Neumeier explains how to bridge this gap to create a clear, differentiated, and innovative brand.

4. **Contagious: How to Build Word of Mouth in the Digital Age by Jonah Berger**
   - √ Discover the science behind why certain products and ideas go viral, and how you can create content and campaigns that drive brand awareness and growth.

5. **Shoe Dog by Phil Knight**
   - √ A memoir by the co-founder of Nike, detailing how the brand grew from a small business to one of the most iconic brands in the world. Knight's journey shows the importance of persistence, storytelling, and vision in building a brand.

6. **Purple Cow: Transform Your Business by Being Remarkable by Seth Godin**
   - √ Godin explains why the key to successful branding is creating something truly remarkable. This book highlights the importance of standing out in a crowded marketplace and how to do it.

7. **Made to Stick: Why Some Ideas Survive and Others Die by Chip Heath and Dan Heath**
   - √ A deep dive into why some ideas (and brands) thrive, while others don't. The Heath brothers provide a framework for creating messages that are memorable, impactful, and sticky.

8. **Zag: The #1 Strategy of High-Performance Brands by Marty Neumeier**
   - √ This follow-up to *Brand Gap* focuses on how brands can differentiate themselves in an oversaturated marketplace. Neumeier argues that when everyone else zigs, you should zag.
9. **The Lean Startup by Eric Ries**
   - √ While primarily a guide to startup growth, this book also emphasizes how branding is essential from day one. Ries outlines how a strong brand can help startups build customer loyalty and pivot when necessary.
10. **The 22 Immutable Laws of Branding by Al Ries and Laura Ries**
    - √ This classic guide offers timeless rules for building and maintaining a successful brand. Al Ries, the father of positioning, outlines the fundamental principles of branding that applies to all businesses.

BRANDING TOOLS AND PLATFORMS

1. **Canva**
   - √ A powerful design tool that allows non-designers to create professional-quality marketing materials, including social media posts, logos, and presentations that maintain brand consistency.
2. **Brand24**
   - √ A social media monitoring tool that tracks mentions of your brand across the web, helping you measure brand sentiment, identify influencers, and manage your brand's reputation.

3. **Hotjar**
   - √ A platform that provides visual insights into how customers interact with your website, helping you optimize the user experience and ensure brand consistency across digital touchpoints.
4. **Ahrefs**
   - √ A comprehensive SEO tool that helps you improve your brand's visibility online by analyzing your website's performance, content, and backlinks.
5. **Loomly**
   - √ A social media management platform that helps brands plan, create, and schedule social media content to maintain a cohesive brand voice across multiple platforms.

ONLINE BRANDING COURSES AND TRAINING
1. **Skillshare**
   - ○ Skillshare offers a range of courses focused on branding, storytelling, and marketing strategies. Top branding professionals share practical knowledge in short, actionable lessons.
   - √ **Udemy**
     - √ Udemy provides in-depth courses on branding, including topics like personal branding, digital marketing, and building a strong online presence for small businesses and startups.
2. **LinkedIn Learning**
   - √ This platform offers a wide variety of courses on branding, including personal branding,

social media strategies, and building a recognizable brand.

BRANDING PODCASTS AND YOUTUBE CHANNELS

1. **The Brand Builder Podcast**
   - √ This podcast covers everything from product development to scaling your brand, with actionable insights from top entrepreneurs and brand builders.

2. **Marketing Over Coffee**
   - √ A podcast that blends branding, content marketing, and social media strategies to help you stay up to date with modern branding trends.

3. **The Futur YouTube Channel**
   - √ Led by Chris Do, this channel offers free lessons on branding, design, and creative entrepreneurship, with a focus on growing your personal and business brand.

4. **On Branding Podcast**
   - √ On Branding features interviews with top brand strategists and experts, diving deep into what it takes to build, grow, and maintain strong brands in today's marketplace.

5. **HBR IdeaCast**
   - √ While not exclusively about branding, this Harvard Business Review podcast often covers branding in the context of business strategy, leadership, and innovation. It features interviews with top business minds, including branding and marketing experts.

6. **The Ground Up Show**
   - √ Hosted by filmmaker Matt D'Avella, this YouTube channel dives into the stories of entrepreneurs, creators, and brands that started from nothing. It focuses on the importance of brand storytelling and connecting with your audience authentically.
7. **Call to Action Podcast by Unbounce**
   - √ This podcast focuses on actionable insights for marketers, with frequent deep dives into branding strategies. Topics include brand positioning, creating emotional connections with audiences, and integrating branding into digital marketing efforts.

BRAND COMMUNITIES AND NETWORKING

1. **Behance**
   - √ A community of creative professionals where you can showcase your branding work, get inspiration, and connect with potential collaborators or clients.
2. **Branding & Marketing Group on LinkedIn**
   - √ This LinkedIn group provides a space for marketers, brand managers, and entrepreneurs to share insights, ask questions, and stay updated on the latest branding trends.
3. **BrandNew**
   - √ An online community and blog that focuses on the latest in branding, logo design, and identity work, providing inspiration and updates on major brand changes globally.

AI TOOLS FOR BRANDING AND MARKETING

1. **Copy.ai**
   - √ An AI-driven writing assistant that helps you create compelling marketing copy, slogans, and brand messaging, making it easier to maintain a consistent brand voice.

2. **Descript**
   - √ A tool that offers AI-powered video and audio editing, allowing you to create branded multimedia content for podcasts, webinars, and video marketing.

3. **ManyChat**
   - √ A conversational marketing platform that allows you to automate brand messaging on social platforms, helping you build stronger relationships with customers.

4. **HubSpot CRM**
   - √ A powerful CRM tool that allows you to manage customer interactions, track engagement, and maintain brand consistency through personalized messaging.

ABOUT THE AUTHOR

Karee Laing is a bold and visionary marketing strategist, branding expert, and the founder of a highly successful marketing agency. Known for her unique blend of creativity and strategic thinking, Karee has helped hundreds of businesses craft standout brands that connect deeply with their audiences. Her journey into the world of branding was an unconventional one—starting as an "accidental entrepreneur" after law school, Karee's passion for storytelling and visual design propelled her into the creative world.

Karee began her marketing career in the automotive industry, but it wasn't until her role expanded into the design/build industry, where she quickly realized the power of branding in shaping perceptions and driving success. This led her to start her own business, where she

utilized her keen eye for visual storytelling to help clients build impactful brands. Her breakthrough came with a major branding project for a global oil and gas company, and from there, she's continued to grow her agency, earning over 100 industry awards for her work.

With a deep understanding of the psychology behind branding, Karee's approach blends authenticity, emotional connection, and strategy to create brands that not only stand out but resonate on a personal level. She is passionate about helping entrepreneurs, startups, and small business owners build brands that are memorable, meaningful, and profitable.

Karee's work has been featured in various industry publications, and she continues to mentor the next generation of entrepreneurs through her insights on branding, storytelling, and innovation. Her mission is simple: to help businesses transform their brands into powerful assets that lead to lasting success.

www.ingramcontent.com/pod-product-compliance
Lightning Source LLC
Chambersburg PA
CBHW030457210326
41597CB00013B/701

Thank You
for Reading My Book

Thank you for reading my book and taking the time to invest in your brand's future. I hope the insights, strategies, and suggestions have inspired you to create something truly meaningful and impactful. Your brand has the power to connect, inspire, and transform—so keep moving forward with confidence and creativity.

I'd love to hear your thoughts! If you have any suggestions or insights on how this book could be improved, or topics you'd like to see explored further, please feel free to share. Your feedback is invaluable in helping me make future editions even better.

thank you!
Karee ♥